# NEW ENGLAND PATRIOTS

## YESTERDAY & TODAY ™

RICHARD A. JOHNSON
FOREWORD BY STEVE GROGAN

WEST
SIDE
PUBLISHING

**Richard A. Johnson** has served as the curator of The Sports Museum in Boston since 1982. In that time, the Bates College graduate has written, co-written, or edited nearly 20 sports books, including histories of several Major League Baseball teams. Johnson is also the author of *A Century of Boston Sports* and recently teamed up with his son, Robert H. Johnson, to write books on the Boston Celtics and the Boston Marathon.

**Steve Grogan** played with the New England Patriots for 16 seasons, which is still a franchise record. During that time he amassed more than 25,000 passing yards and, although injured in the playoffs, was a key member of the 1985 AFC championship team. His outstanding career earned him a spot on the team's 35th anniversary squad, as well as induction into the Patriots' Hall of Fame.

Factual verification by Karl Hente.

Publications International, Ltd., would like to thank the Kraft family and the Patriots organization for granting us access to the artifacts and memorabilia at The Hall at Patriot Place. We would especially like to acknowledge Brent Hensel, curator of The Hall, and Robyn Glaser, senior advisor for the Kraft Group, for helping us arrange and carry out a successful photo shoot at The Hall.

We would also like to thank Jim Mahoney, Martha Reagan, and Alan Thibeault of the *Boston Herald;* Aaron Schmidt of the Boston Public Library, Print Department; and Richard A. Johnson, who doubled as author and memorabilia provider, supplying numerous items from his vast coffers of Patriots ephemera.

Yesterday & Today is a trademark of Publications International, Ltd.

West Side Publishing is a division of Publications International, Ltd.

Copyright © 2009 Publications International, Ltd. All rights reserved. This book may not be reproduced or quoted in whole or in part by any means whatsoever without written permission from:

Louis Weber, CEO
Publications International, Ltd.
7373 North Cicero Avenue
Lincolnwood, Illinois 60712

Permission is never granted for commercial purposes.

ISBN-13: 978-1-4124-9828-9
ISBN-10: 1-4127-9828-0

Manufactured in China.

8 7 6 5 4 3 2 1

Library of Congress Control Number: 2009924978

Front cover: **Getty Images** (top left, top right & left center); *Sports Illustrated/*Getty Images (top center & right center)

Back cover: **AP Images** (left, right center & right); **Getty Images** (left center)

**Al Ruelle Collection**: 29 (right); **AP Images**: contents, endsheets, 3, 16 (bottom), 19 (top), 24 (right), 25 (left), 27, 28 (left), 30 (top center), 31 (bottom right), 34–35, 41 (bottom left), 46, 50 (top), 53, 63 (top), 67, 71 (bottom), 73, 75 (top), 85 (top), 88 (bottom), 95 (top left & bottom), 98 (right), 100, 106, 107 (bottom), 109 (top), 110 (top), 114, 116 (bottom), 117 (top), 123 (top), 126 (left), 127 (top), 133 (bottom), 139 (bottom), 141 (top), 143, 148 (bottom), 151 (top), 154 (top), 155 (top); **Boston Herald:** 10, 11, 13 (top), 23 (bottom right), 30 (bottom center), 32 (right), 47 (top), 52, 55 (right), 60 (right), 64 (bottom), 65 (top), 69 (top left), 70, 76 (top right), 79 (bottom), 82 (top), 88 (top), 91, 101, 105 (top right), 115, 116 (top), 117 (bottom), 118, 119, 121 (bottom center), 122 (top), 126 (right), 130, 131, 132, 133 (top), 134 (top center), 136, 137, 138, 140, 141 (bottom), 142, 144, 145 (top), 146 (top center), 150, 152 (top left); **Boston Public Library, Print Department:** 18 (top); Photos courtesy *Boston Herald/Herald Traveler,* 15 (bottom center), 20 (right), 36 (left); **Chris Beaudoin Photography, Boston, MA. Photographs taken and used courtesy The Hall at Patriot Place Presented by Raytheon:** 8 (left), 14 (top left & left center), 18 (right), 30 (left), 31 (top left & top right), 36 (right), 40 (bottom right), 41 (top left), 43 (left), 48 (top right), 58 (bottom), 62 (top right), 76 (top center), 89 (bottom), 104 (bottom left), 112 (bottom left), 121 (top center), 124 (left), 134 (bottom), 135 (bottom right), 153 (top right), 155 (bottom right); © **Corbis:** 12, 43 (right), 51; Bettmann, 8–9, 26 (top), 47 (bottom); Rick Friedman, 107 (top); Robert Klein/Icon Sports Media, 87 (bottom left); Brian Snyder/Reuters, 113 (top right); **Getty Images:** 18 (left), 19 (bottom), 38 (bottom), 39, 42, 44 (right), 58 (top), 64 (top), 74 (right), 96–97, 98 (left), 102 (right), 103, 110 (bottom), 111 (bottom right), 120 (bottom right), 123 (bottom), 124–25, 148 (top), 149; AFP, 80–81, 94 (top), 109 (bottom left), 111 (bottom left); MLB Photos, 20 (left); *Sports Illustrated,* contents, 17, 45 (right), 54 (right), 75 (bottom left), 84 (bottom), 85 (bottom left), 99 (top), 122 (bottom), 128, 129, 155 (bottom left); Time Life Pictures, 89 (top), 99 (bottom right); **NFL:** 29 (left), 38 (top), 44 (left), 56–57, 68 (bottom right), 71 (top), 72, 78 (bottom), 90 (left), 108; **PIL Collection:** contents, 6 (bottom), 13 (bottom), 14 (top right & bottom right), 15 (top & bottom left), 16 (top), 22 (top center & right), 23 (top left & top right), 24 (left), 28 (right), 30 (top right), 31 (bottom left), 32 (left), 33, 34, 37, 40 (top left & top right), 41 (top right & bottom right), 48 (bottom right), 49 (top right, top left & bottom right), 50 (bottom), 55 (left), 62 (top left, left center & right center), 63 (bottom left & bottom right), 65 (bottom), 66, 68 (top left, top right & bottom left), 69 (top right, bottom right & bottom left), 76 (bottom center), 77 (left center & right center), 79 (top), 80, 83 (bottom), 84 (top), 85 (bottom right), 86 (center, top left & bottom right), 87 (top right, bottom center & bottom right), 90 (right), 92, 93 (top left), 94 (bottom), 95 (top right), 96, 99 (bottom left), 102 (left), 104 (top left, top right & bottom right), 105 (top left, bottom left & bottom right), 111 (top), 112 (top left & top center), 113 (top left & top center), 120 (top left, top right & bottom left), 121 (top right & left center), 127 (bottom), 134 (top left), 135 (top left, top right & bottom left), 145 (bottom), 146 (left, right & bottom), 147 (top left, bottom left & bottom right), 151 (bottom), 152 (top right, bottom left & bottom center), 153 (top left, bottom left & bottom right), 154 (bottom), 157, 158; **Richard A. Johnson Collection:** 14 (bottom right), 15 (right), 21, 22 (top left & bottom center), 23 (bottom left & bottom center), 25 (right), 26 (bottom), 38 (left), 40 (bottom left), 45 (left), 48 (top left), 49 (bottom left), 56, 63 (bottom center), 74 (left), 75 (bottom right), 76 (top left), 77 (top left & top center), 82 (bottom), 86 (bottom left), 87 (top left), 93 (top right & bottom right), 109 (bottom right), 112 (right), 113 (bottom left), 134 (right), 147 (top right), 152 (bottom right); **Steve Grogan Collection:** 6 (left), 7; **Tom Croke/Visual Image, Inc., www.visualimageinc.com:** 48 (bottom left), 54 (left), 59, 60 (left), 61, 78 (top), 83 (top), 93 (bottom left), 139 (top)

Additional memorabilia photography: PDR Productions, Inc./Peter Rossi

*Adam Vinatieri jumps for joy as his 48-yard field goal clinches the Patriots' first-ever Super Bowl victory. The Pats upset the St. Louis Rams on February 3, 2002.*

# Contents

*Kicker Gino Cappelletti*

*1961 Patriots program*

*John Hannah*

*Andre Tippett*

*Super Bowl XXXVIII banner*

*Tom Brady*

# *Foreword*

## BY STEVE GROGAN

When my career with the New England Patriots ended after the 1990 season, I finally had time to look back and see what had happened during my professional football career. No one would have guessed when I arrived as an unheralded quarterback out of Kansas State in 1975 that I would leave 16 years later as the longest-tenured Patriot to this day. I've realized that it took not only hard work and dedication to the game but also some breaks and good luck along the way.

I was fortunate to play for some coaches that recognized certain talents that I had on the football field and permitted me to use those talents. Chuck Fairbanks, my first head coach, let me use my running ability. Ron Erhardt, my second head coach, saw that I could call my own game. He taught me how it was done and then turned me loose. The result was that I had some of my better years under that system in the NFL. Coach Raymond Berry took that process to the next level and not only allowed me to call the plays when I was on the field, but also asked me to make calls for the other quarterbacks who were in the game.

*Steve Grogan*

In order to last as long as I did, you have to have great teammates. I was fortunate to play with three Pro Football Hall of Famers. Perhaps the greatest guard ever was John Hannah. Mike Haynes was a cornerback who split his career with the Patriots and the Oakland Raiders. The third was Andre Tippett, who was a dominant outside linebacker. Other outstanding teammates included several players who are now in the Patriots' Hall of Fame. Steve Nelson was our great middle linebacker. Stanley Morgan was my favorite receiver. Bruce Armstrong, a fine left tackle, was with us late in my career. A number of excellent players also wore Patriot uniforms from 1975 to 1990—too many to name.

I think the 1976 squad was perhaps the best Patriot team I played on. We had a great blend of veteran leadership and some young players that were very talented and became the nucleus of the organization for the successful run in the late '70s. Had it not been for a questionable roughing-the-passer call in our playoff game against Oakland, I believe this would have been the first Patriot Super Bowl championship team. We were a close-knit bunch, which made it a lot of fun to be a part of that team.

The 1985 team became the first Patriot team to reach the Super Bowl. It was an interesting group, playing under first-year head coach Raymond Berry. The fact that we made it to the Super Bowl was surprising. After a slow start, Tony Eason, who was starting at quarterback at the time, was injured. I came off the bench for the first time in more than a year and played probably the best football I had ever played. It was a magical run, and we won six games in a row.

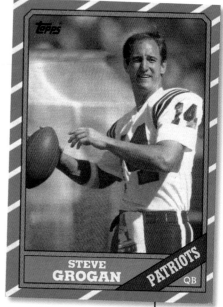

*Steve Grogan's 1986 Topps football card*

movers and shakers of the turbulent '60s. In a decade that produced such rebels as Jimi Hendrix, Eldridge Cleaver, Eugene McCarthy, Gloria Steinem, and Timothy Leary, these executives challenged the preeminence of the National Football League and made their mark with the Spalding J5V football.

The tapered contours of the J5V came to symbolize all that was great about the new league. This was a football made for passing. Unlike their counterparts in the NFL, who seemed content to perpetuate their rough-hewn image of smashmouth "three yards and a cloud of dust" football, the new league took to the air with a style that shook the sport to its tradition-bound foundations.

*Former Notre Dame publicist and Patriots owner Billy Sullivan* (center) *presents a silver Revere Bowl to legendary Notre Dame football coach Frank Leahy* (right). *Dallas Texans owner Lamar Hunt stands with them prior to the Pats' first exhibition game on August 14, 1960.*

The lasting image of the league, and one that remains strong to this day, is that of the sport as imagined by Chargers head coach Sid Gillman, who thought nothing of asking quarterbacks Tobin Rote and John Hadl to throw the ball up to 40 times per game.

Simply put, the new league was a renegade operation. Not only were the owners a collection of stylish (but wealthy) rejects, but their coaches and players also comprised nothing less than a last-chance saloon of suspects and prospects culled from the NFL waiver wire, the Canadian Football League, and college and sandlot teams.

Apart from giving countless players a second chance at professional football, the new league also gave cities like Denver, Buffalo, Houston, Oakland, and later Kansas City and San Diego their first major-league sports opportunity of any kind. Although each of these markets had appeared on the radar screen of the NFL as possible expansion locales, the new league acted with speed and guile. Nevertheless, they did lose the Minnesota market only after a last-minute ambush by the NFL.

Armed with a television contract that paid each franchise $300,000, the AFL more than held its own. Among the college stars to sign with the new league were Charlie Flowers, Johnny Robinson, and Billy Cannon. And, while credibility came gradually, the new league soon attracted a rogues' gallery of unforgettable characters such as Al Davis, Ben Davidson, Johnny Sample, Cookie Gilchrist, Jack Kemp, and Joe Namath.

Within ten years this league of outsiders did more to change football than anybody since Walter Camp. Not only was their product more entertaining than that of the NFL, but their back-to-back victories in Super Bowls III and IV also led many to question whether the AFL was merging into the NFL or if it wasn't the other way around.

# Here Come the Patriots!

The late 1950s was a period of stark contrasts in the world of professional sports in Boston. The Red Sox were still princes of a shrinking city. While enjoying the cheers of capacity Boston Garden crowds, the Bruins had to scuffle just to make the playoffs. The Celtics had just secured the services of Bill Russell and were about to embark on the greatest journey ever taken by any North American pro sports team, winning 11 NBA titles in 13 seasons. Professional football was merely an afterthought, a relic from the past preserved in the pages of old scrapbooks that detailed the exploits of the proud but defunct Braves, Shamrocks, Redskins, and Yanks.

It was in this atmosphere that Boston oil executive Billy Sullivan stepped into the picture. For a time he explored the possibility of purchasing the Chicago Cardinals of the NFL and moving them to Boston, but the Cardinals decided to move to St. Louis. Sullivan then heard that the proposed AFL needed an eighth franchise. In no time he made the appropriate contacts and scrambled to raise the $25,000 franchise fee due within 48 hours of the phone call granting him the contract.

The tale of the 1960 Boston Patriots is that of an offbeat epic with a cast of hundreds. Head coach Lou Saban estimated that more than 350 players tried out for his team. Among their number were countless NFL rejects and former college and Canadian Football League hotshots. Former Michigan State quarterback Tom Yewcic recalled, "The guys you dressed next to for the morning practice were different than the guys who dressed for the afternoon practices. We had three teams at any given time: one coming, one going, and one playing."

During that inaugural season, the Patriots played most of their home games on Friday nights, with their first game on September 9, 1960, which was also the first-ever AFL contest. In a painful preview of coming attractions, the Patriots lost this historic game to Denver by a score of 13–10, despite the fact that Gino Cappelletti scored the first three points in league history on a first-quarter field goal. Only later did the team learn that Broncos coach Frank Filchock had watched their practice the day before and therefore knew more about his opponent's offense than any Patriot lineman.

Although the Patriots went 5–9 and finished in fourth place, they filled a glaring void in Boston's sports calendar and attracted crowds that averaged nearly 17,000.

*On February 8, 1960, the Boston Patriots appointed Lou Saban (pictured) to be their first head coach, a position he held until Mike Holovak replaced him on October 10, 1961. Previously he was an All-Big Ten quarterback and fullback for the University of Indiana and coached at Northwestern and Western Illinois. After leaving the Patriots, he led the Buffalo Bills to AFL championships in 1964 and 1965.*

# Ron Burton's Legacy

**W**hen the Patriots selected Northwestern University all-purpose back Ron Burton as their first-ever draft choice, they welcomed a man who would become one of their top players and would also establish himself as one of New England's most beloved citizens.

Burton hailed from Springfield, Ohio, where he had raised himself as an orphan following the death of his mother and departure of his father during his sophomore year of high school. Always a talented athlete, Burton followed a spartan training regimen that included lights-out at 7:30 P.M. and rising at 4:00 A.M. for a 7.5-mile run prior to finishing his schoolwork.

Following a sensational senior season, Burton was considered the best high school player in football-mad Ohio. Among his 47 college scholarship offers was a personal appeal from coach Woody Hayes to join his Ohio State Buckeye squad. Not only did Burton reject Hayes's attractive offer, but he also stunned many by choosing to attend Big Ten doormat Northwestern University.

Guided by head coach Ara Parseghian, Burton helped lead the Wildcats from a 0–9 record as a sophomore to top national ranking in his final two seasons, with victories against Ohio State, Michigan, Oklahoma, and Notre Dame. He remains one of only four consensus All-Americans in the history of Northwestern football.

Injuries, however, marked his Patriot career, which led coach Mike Holovak to remark in his book, *Violence Every Sunday,* "Burton would have been one of the all-time greats, but he was unlucky physically. Everything happened to him."

RON BURTON
HALFBACK • BOSTON PATRIOTS

*Running back Ron Burton will forever be recognized as both the first Patriot draft choice and as one of Boston's greatest citizens.*

*Northwestern star running back Ron Burton displays a No. 1 jersey, signifying his status as the Patriots' first overall draft choice in the first-ever American Football League draft.*

Despite his many setbacks, Burton still managed a career rushing total of 1,536 yards, for an average of 3.6 yards per carry. He became the first Patriot to rush for more than 100 yards in a game against Denver on October 23, 1960, and he enjoyed a breakthrough season in 1962, gaining a total of 1,009 yards (rushing and receiving).

Following his playing career, Burton ascended the corporate ladder at John Hancock Mutual Life Insurance Company. But more important, he became a local legend after building the Ron Burton Training Village, a facility located on 300 acres in Hubbardston, Massachusetts, which teaches life skills to boys between the ages of 11 and 19. Burton died of cancer in 2003, and to date several thousand young men have completed the program that stands as the lasting legacy of the first Patriot.

# PATRIOTS PANORAMA

This is the drawing of the original Patriots helmet logo that was sent to Billy Sullivan by Walter Pingree. The Patriots used this logo for their first season. The helmet is a replica of that used by the Patriots during the 1960 season.

The "Pat Patriot" logo appears on this replica of a 1960 pennant. The old logo has remained a fixture on the merchandise sold at the team's mammoth ProShop at Patriot Place.

This Boston Patriots pin replaced the Boston Yanks and Boston Redskins souvenirs that came before it in the collections of Boston's loyal corps of pro football fans.

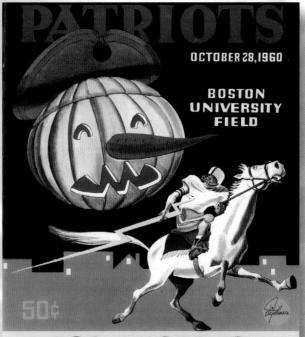

The early Patriots program covers, drawn by cartoonists Phil Bissell and Vic Johnson, are among the most collectible of AFL artifacts due to their often humorous subjects and vivid colors. Johnson drew the cover on this program.

This Patriots pin commemorates the founding of the team in 1960. Some fans viewed the "Flying Elvis" logo with suspicion upon its arrival in the early 1990s, but now it's the symbol of the franchise's Super Bowl victories.

Astute fans recognized the resemblance between the cartoon Houston Oiler on this program cover and Oilers chairman Bud Adams. Pat Patriot appears in the window of a representation of Paul Revere's Boston birthplace.

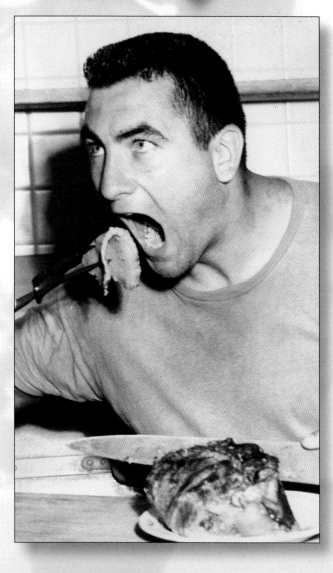

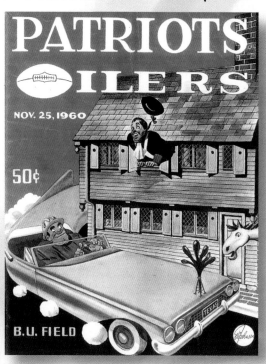

Part of the appeal of the AFL was the light touch given to details on game programs. The league stood in stark contrast to the image of the NFL, aka the "No Fun League."

All-AFL defensive end Larry Eisenhauer was nothing less than a class clown. In this posed photo, he holds a carving knife while gulping a large slice of meat at the 1961 Patriots training camp.

# Mr. Patriot

Gino Cappelletti may be the greatest player not yet enshrined in the Pro Football Hall of Fame in Canton, Ohio. Not only does the versatile kicker/wide receiver forever reign as the all-time scoring leader of the American Football League, but he is also one of only three players, along with George Blanda and Jim Otto, to have played in every AFL regular-season game.

Cappelletti has remained a Patriot for most of the team's existence, taking time away from the game to work in business prior to returning as an assistant coach and now as the team's radio color commentator. He is as beloved a figure to Patriots fans as Phil Rizzuto is to the Yankees, Ron Santo to the Cubs, and Johnny Pesky to the Red Sox Nation. Known to all as "The Duke," Cappelletti savors the recent triumphs of his team while

Fans knew the AFL had made it to the mainstream of American sports when the venerable Topps Chewing Gum Company began printing their trading cards and when NBC, with Curt Gowdy, began broadcasting their games. This Topps card from 1965 shows Gino Cappelletti in a catching pose.

more than earning his regal nickname by serving as the living symbol of, and elder statesman for, his many AFL teammates.

When news of the formation of the American Football League reached the former University of Minnesota quarterback in the spring of 1960, Cappelletti was tending bar and playing touch football in Minneapolis. It had been half a dozen years since Cappelletti had starred at the university, and his football career had taken him to a wide array of teams. Included in this journey were several stints in the Canadian Football League, time with the army team at Fort Sill, Oklahoma, and an unsuccessful tryout with the Detroit Lions.

At age 27, with his athletic options dwindling, Cappelletti was at first over-looked by Patriots coach Lou Saban, who traveled to the Twin Cities to scout and sign several of Cappelletti's former Minnesota teammates and current touch football buddies. In an interview with sportswriter George Sullivan, Cappelletti noted, "There were two voices in my head. One said to forget it, it wasn't meant to be, and the other argued to give it one more try."

Cappelletti made several calls and tracked Saban to his home in Illinois. While pleading his case to the former Northwestern coach, he even offered to pay his own expenses to Massachusetts if it meant getting a tryout. Upon his arrival at training camp, the former quarterback announced his intention to kick and play

*Gino Cappelletti retired as the all-time leading scorer in AFL history, with 1,100 points scored in double duty as a wide receiver and place-kicker. He is shown here kicking an extra point in his 24-point effort against the Buffalo Bills on November 15, 1964.*

defensive back. In five exhibition games, his defensive prowess earned him a roster spot, and his kicking improved with each game.

On September 9, 1960, Cappelletti made football history when he kicked the first points in AFL history with a first-quarter, 34-yard field goal during the game against the Broncos in Boston. In the Patriots' 13–10 loss, he also lost his job as defensive back—but soon was back by serving the team as its most versatile player.

At practice one afternoon, Cappelletti stepped in for an injured wide receiver. Assistant coach Mike Holovak, a man known for his sharp eye for talent, liked his moves and soft hands. Cappelletti kept practicing and even started at wide receiver for the last game of the team's inaugural season, catching one pass.

*Former University of Minnesota star Gino Cappelletti led the fledgling American Football League in scoring five times. Here he is in action against the Buffalo Bills in 1962.*

The 1961 season proved to be the ultimate test of Cappelletti's strength and adaptability as he fought back from a severe case of hepatitis. The growing pile of medical bills and the fact that Saban had informed him that he'd lost his kicking duties to former Syracuse star Bob Yates served as powerful incentives for a make-or-break training camp.

In the Patriots' final exhibition game in Buffalo, Cappelletti caught a touchdown pass from quarterback Babe Parilli and watched as Yates's point-after attempt was blocked. Later in the game, Coach Saban put Cappelletti back in as kicker and was rewarded with three field goals from 32, 35, and 38 yards, the last field goal coming with only 30 seconds remaining in a tied game.

His career restored, Cappelletti enjoyed a breakout season that year, catching eight touchdowns while kicking 17 field goals and 48 extra points to lead the AFL in scoring. It was the first of six straight seasons in which he scored 100 or more points. That record wasn't even approachable until the Patriots' own Adam Vinatieri reached the century mark in ten straight seasons.

Amazingly enough, Cappelletti's 155 points in 1964 and 147 points in 1961 remain the second- and third-highest point totals in AFL/NFL history. He enjoyed his greatest season in 1964, leading the Patriots to a 10–3–1 record and capturing league MVP honors.

In 1992, the Patriots retired his No. 20 when he was named to the team's Hall of Fame.

# The First Team

The 1960 Patriots possessed a homespun quality that permeated all aspects of their operation. Not only did their fans name them in a contest, but Walter Pingree also designed their first helmet logo, which depicted a colonial tricornered hat. Pingree was a New England railroad conductor and amateur artist who had included his drawing in a fan letter mailed to team president Billy Sullivan.

On June 17, players participated in a motorcade through Charlestown in celebration of Bunker Hill Day. Five days later the Patriots announced their first exhibition game—a benefit for mentally challenged children—against the Dallas Texans at Harvard Stadium. That same day, the Patriots held an open tryout at St. Sebastian's School in Newton. Of the 72 sandlot stars and former collegians who tried out, head coach Lou Saban signed seven and informed the press that he expected more than 100 players to attend his upcoming training camp. By the end of camp, more than three times that number had been put through their paces by the fledgling team.

Their original lineup was filled with familiar faces, such as 36-year-old quarterback Butch Songin. Songin, a former Boston College standout, took leave from his job as a probation officer to have one last crack at pro football. Considered by many to have been the finest collegiate hockey player of his

*Everett, Massachusetts, native Ross O'Hanley played safety for the Boston Patriots from 1960 to 1965 and earned an All-AFL selection in his first season.*

*Ed "Butch" Songin was a star quarterback at Boston College. He quarterbacked the Patriots in their first two seasons.*

generation, Songin enjoyed an outstanding return to football, achieving a solid quarterback rating of 70.9 while tossing 22 touchdowns in 14 games.

Among Songin's 53 teammates, nine had attended local colleges, including five from Boston College, two from rival Holy Cross, and one each from Dartmouth and Brandeis.

On September 9, the Patriots played their first regular-season game in AFL history against the Denver Broncos before 20,000 fans at newly refurbished Boston University Field, on the site of old Braves Field. They lost by a narrow 13–10 score, courtesy of a brilliant 76-yard punt return by Bronco Gene Mingo. The Patriots then won two of their next three games before slogging through a campaign that saw them win only three of their remaining ten games.

Among the highlights of their first season was their home attendance, which averaged just under 17,000—including a sellout crowd of 27,123 for their November 25 game against Houston—and bested the average home attendance of both the New York Titans and Los Angeles Chargers. In addition, linebacker Tom Addison and safety Ross O'Hanley were named to the league's first All-Star team, while defensive lineman Bob Dee and guard Charlie Leo made the second team. The team had survived against great odds. The league, however, with its wide-open style of play, was only beginning to win the hearts and minds of Boston football fans.

*This distinctive football-shape ticket stub is from the Pats' first-ever regular-season home game, played at Boston University on September 9, 1960.*

# The Eagles' Nest

**P**atriots founder Billy Sullivan, from the Boston College class of '37, was much like his college friend, future House Speaker Thomas "Tip" O'Neill, who famously pronounced that "all politics is local." So, apparently, was building a football team, for Sullivan included no fewer than 11 Boston College alumni on his first ten Patriot teams.

Led by former Eagle quarterback Ed "Butch" Songin, the first Patriot team also featured Eagles fullback Alan Miller, offensive end Joe Johnson, safety Ross O'Hanley, and wide receiver Jim Colclough.

Colclough, who grew up in Quincy, was a genuine hometown hero. In his rookie year of 1960, he led the Pats with 49 receptions for 666 yards and nine touchdowns. During his nine-year career, he compiled 283 receptions for 5,001 yards, which stood as a team record until 1983, when Stanley Morgan surpassed him. Colclough remains among the top five in team history for receiving yards, receiving touchdowns, and average yards per reception.

Included on the honor roll of the 27 Boston College alumni to have played for the Patriots to date are Heisman Trophy winner Doug Flutie, Outland Trophy winner Mike Ruth, and unique characters like former All-Pro Fred Smerlas and Larry Eisenhauer.

Eisenhauer was known to teammates as "Ike" or "Wildman" for punching lockers, knocking holes into locker room walls with his forearms and helmet, and acting as the team's class clown. In a widely reported incident in 1963, Eisenhauer trotted onto the snowy turf of Kansas City's Municipal Stadium for pregame warm-ups clad in only his helmet and jockstrap.

Today's Patriots are comprised of a far more varied and geographically diverse player pool. Nevertheless, their ties to Boston College were an important factor in their growth and early success.

*Doug Flutie was a folk hero in New England long before his two stints with the Patriots. He is shown in action against the New Orleans Saints at Gillette Stadium on August 18, 2005.*

## BOSTON COLLEGE ALUMNI AS PATRIOTS 1960–TODAY

| | |
|---|---|
| Don Allard, QB, 1962 | Chris Sullivan, DE, 1996–99, 2001 |
| Michael Cloud, RB, 2003, 2005 | Bill Turner, OG, 1987 |
| Jim Colclough, WR, 1960–68 | Darren Twombly, C, 1987 |
| Tom Condon, OG, 1985 | Jim Whalen, TE, 1965–69 |
| Steve Corbett, OG, 1975 | Damien Woody, C, 1999–2003 |
| Harry Crump, RB, 1963 | |
| Steve DeOssie, LB, 1994–95 | |
| Larry Eisenhauer, DE, 1961–69 | |
| Doug Flutie, QB, 1987–89, 2005 | |
| Art Graham, WR, 1963–68 | |
| David Green, RB, 1995 | |
| Bob Hyland, C, 1977 | |
| Joe Johnson, RB/E, 1960–61 | |
| Dan Koppen, C, 2003–present | |
| Alan Miller, RB, 1960 | |
| Ross O'Hanley, DB, 1960–65 | |
| Tom Porell, NT, 1987 | |
| Frank Robotti, LB, 1961 | |
| Mike Ruth, NT, 1986–87 | |
| Fred Smerlas, NT, 1991–92 | |
| Ed "Butch" Songin, QB, 1960–61 | |
| Fred Steinfort, K, 1983 | |

*Defensive end Larry Eisenhauer*

# The Founding Father

**B**illy Sullivan started the Boston Patriots with $8,000, an abundant supply of charm/blarney, and a dogged determination to succeed where four other Boston-based pro football franchises had failed. Upon receiving the news he'd been granted the eighth and final AFL franchise on November 16, 1959, Sullivan used nearly every second of the 48-hour window his fellow owners had given him to raise the required $25,000 to enter the league. Calling friends and relatives on the weekend before Thanksgiving, he just managed to raise the money and secure Boston's first new major-league franchise since the Celtics were founded in 1946.

Such challenges were nothing new to Sullivan, who'd worked his way through Boston College. Upon graduation, he became the sports information director at his alma mater and the primary media contact for head football coach Frank Leahy and his nationally ranked teams.

When Leahy left to coach at Notre Dame in 1941, Sullivan soon followed to help promote and expand the legend and myth of Notre Dame football. It was Sullivan who spearheaded the groundbreaking promotional campaign that secured the 1943 Heisman Trophy for quarterback Angelo Bertelli.

Before long, Sullivan's skills brought him home to Boston, where he worked as the public relations director for the Boston Braves, one of the original Major League Baseball teams, before the club moved to Milwaukee (and then to Atlanta). Among his many crowd-pleasing innovations were the design of

*Few Patriots fans are aware that team founder Billy Sullivan was instrumental in starting the Jimmy Fund of the Dana-Farber Cancer Institute while working as PR director of the Boston Braves. The distinctive Jimmy Fund collection boxes remain a fixture at Fenway Park and a fitting memorial to Sullivan.*

*Patriots owner Billy Sullivan (pictured) fought valiantly, but unsuccessfully, to keep his team in Boston, lobbying politicians such as Boston mayor Kevin White. The Patriots played their final season in Boston and their first in the NFL at Harvard Stadium in 1970.*

luxury box seats, called "sky-views," the improvement of concessions to sell local delicacies such as fried clams, the production of team highlight films (including the first-ever team-sponsored film in color), the creation of an array of promotional events such as fan appreciation day, the publication of annual yearbooks, and the successful promotional campaign that resulted in the election of third baseman Bob Elliott as National League MVP in 1947.

When Braves attendance began to slip in the early 1950s, Sullivan devised a press tour of Braves minor-league teams on a plane nicknamed the "Rookie Rocket." The idea was to expose Boston's sporting press to promising prospects such as future Hall of Famer Eddie Mathews and a young shortstop named Henry Aaron.

Sullivan's greatest achievement, possibly surpassing even his founding of the Patriots, was the creation of the Jimmy Fund as a Braves-sponsored charity in 1947. The world-renowned clinic has raised hundreds of millions of dollars for research and the operation of the world-famous Dana-Farber Cancer Institute.

For a generation, Sullivan, as team owner of the Boston Patriots, made everything about his team a grassroots operation. The Patriots practiced on an enlarged median strip adjacent to Logan Airport in East Boston, called White Stadium, where the team sat on milk crates while viewing game films projected on a bedsheet. Their logo, Pat Patriot, was originally drawn as a sports cartoon by *Boston Globe* cartoonist Phil Bissell and was selected

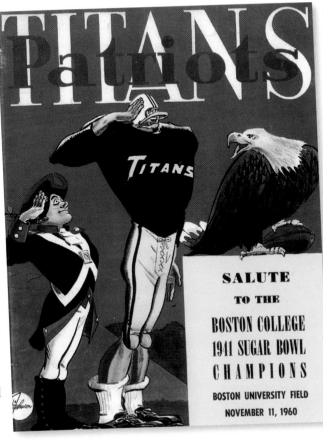

*The Boston Patriots, led by owner and Boston College alumnus Billy Sullivan, never missed an opportunity to tie the new team to the region's glorious football history. On the cover of this Patriots program is a tribute to the 1941 Boston College Sugar Bowl champions.*

by Sullivan's young son Patrick, who broke the deadlock in a late night meeting at the Sullivan home. When Sullivan asked the youngster which design he preferred, Patrick chose the cartoon over the more stylized logos neatly lined up by the assembled advertising executives.

Sullivan's tenure was equal parts Frank Capra script and slapstick comedy. Sullivan moved his team among four stadiums before departing Boston for the greener pastures of Foxboro in 1971. It was in Foxboro where he built what sportswriter Dan Shaughnessy called "the Levittown of American sports." While the concrete and aluminum stadium cost just under $7 million, it also was and remains the site of some of the region's worst traffic jams.

In 1985, Sullivan was faced with the prospect of losing his beloved team in the aftermath of his family's failed concert promotion partnership with singer Michael Jackson and boxing promoter Don King. Lucky to emerge with the shirts on their backs, the Sullivans entertained offers as the team made magic on the gridiron.

For three weekends, the Patriots became football's ultimate road warriors, defying long odds while beating the Jets, Raiders, and Dolphins on their way to their first Super Bowl in January 1986. New England fans embraced their team as never before and afforded Billy Sullivan the opportunity to bask in the spotlight at the eleventh hour. Hollywood couldn't have devised a better script for football's happy warrior.

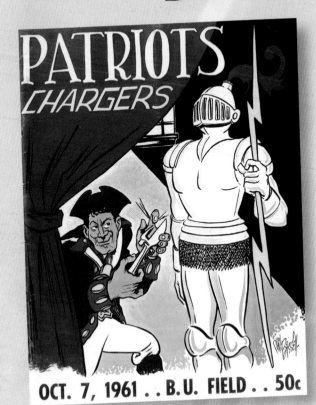

**PATRIOTS** CHARGERS

OCT. 7, 1961 . . B.U. FIELD . . 50¢

Phil Bissell's irreverent Patriot program covers are now sought-after collectibles that connect fans to the humble yet colorful heritage of the Patriot franchise.

The first regular-season game program in AFL history was graced with an illustration of Pat Patriot smacking a Denver Bronco. Bissell's artwork is as much a part of the Patriot franchise's DNA as any Tom Brady touchdown pass.

This car decal displays artist Phil Bissell's "Pat Patriot," which has become an enduring icon of the New England Patriots.

**BOSTON PATRIOTS VS. DENVER BRONCOS**

an invitation for you !!

BOSTON UNIVERSITY FIELD **SEPT. 9th**

50¢

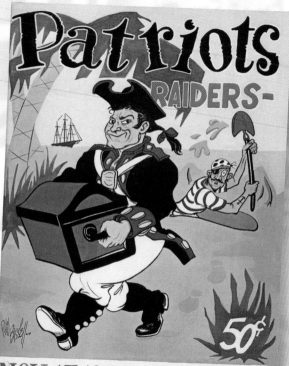

**Patriots** RAIDERS

50¢

NOV. 17, 1961 . . . B.U. FIELD

Long before the Patriots achieved greatness, they were lovable members of a league that enjoyed poking fun at itself while drawing fans with an exciting brand of full-throttle, pass-oriented football.

Once the Patriots started publishing a league-edited program, the Bissell cover images took on a more serious tone. The cartoons were replaced with watercolor sketches of Patriot heroes like quarterback Babe Parilli.

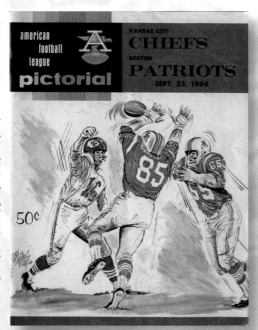

Artist Phil Bissell's autograph is a highly sought-after signature. He depicted the Patriots on game program covers and in the pages of *The Boston Globe* and the *Worcester Evening Gazette*.

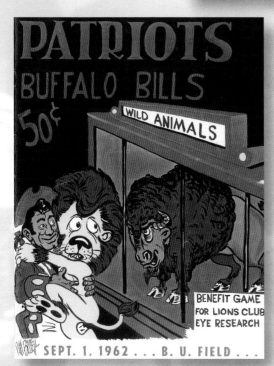

Bissell's reward for creating the team logo was a handshake deal with team owner Billy Sullivan that called for the cartoonist to create the team's home program covers for much of their AFL tenure.

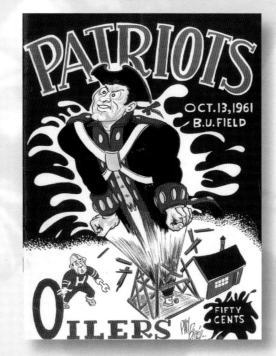

One aspect of the Patriots' off-field success was their affiliation with many local charities, including the Lions Club benefit touted by this delightful Bissell program cover.

Phil Bissell created the "Pat Patriot" logo in a 1959 editorial cartoon drawn for *The Boston Globe*. The football-hiking figure became the team's first logo. That icon, as well as his popular program covers, made Bissell himself an icon among New Englanders.

# The Contenders

*I*n sports, as in life, the old cliché "what goes around comes around" is nothing less than scripture. In 1963, the Boston Patriots fell victim to the sort of skullduggery for which Bill Belichick and his staff were accused in the infamous "Spygate" episode of 2007. In the case of the Patriots' ill-fated trip to San Diego in January 1964 to play the Chargers for the American Football League championship, the past was indeed a prelude to Spygate.

The fate of this Patriots team was especially cruel, as they had just completed one of the more improbable playoff runs in professional football history. They finished the regular season with a respectable 7–6–1 record, which tied them with the Buffalo Bills for the Eastern Division crown. Because there were no wild cards or multitiered playoff setups at the time, only the division champs played in the postseason. Hence, the Patriots' season was extended with a tiebreaking game on December 28, 1963, against the Bills at Buffalo's derelict War Memorial Stadium.

In snowy conditions better suited to ice fishing than football, the Patriots thrashed the Bills by a score of 26–8 on a field covered with pockets of ice. Coach Mike Holovak had prepared his team for the conditions and had running back Larry

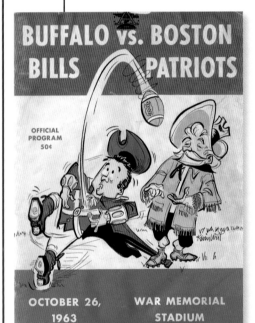

*The old War Memorial Stadium in Buffalo, nicknamed "The Rockpile," always presented a challenge to opposing teams with its hard turf and chilly temperature. While the Patriots lost the game depicted on this program, they defeated the Bills in Buffalo later that season to earn a trip to the AFL title game in San Diego.*

Garron wear baseball spikes for added traction. Not only did Garron score two touchdowns on passes from Babe Parilli, but Gino Cappelletti also kicked four field goals after quickly trading his cleats for sneakers prior to each kick.

In San Diego, the Chargers held light practices during the holiday season while waiting for their bruised challengers. Head coach Sid Gillman had assembled a superb team led by quarterback Tobin Rote, wide receiver Lance Alworth, guard Ron Mix, and running backs Paul Lowe and Keith Lincoln. Despite their depth and the fact that they finished with both an imposing 11–3 record and the best offense and best defense in the league, they had beaten the Patriots by only four points at home and by a single point at Fenway Park.

As he contemplated the prospect of the San Diego Chargers winning their first AFL championship, Gillman would leave nothing to chance. In the seemingly best time-honored tradition of gamesmanship, he contacted Patriot head coach Mike Holovak and offered to set up the Patriots' training facilities at a local naval base.

*Boston Globe* reporter Will McDonough, in an interview with *Dallas Morning News* sportswriter Jeff Miller, recalled, "Mike Holovak was like the nicest

*In 1985, former Patriots head coach Mike Holovak was elected to the College Football Hall of Fame on the merits of his outstanding career at Boston College during the Frank Leahy era.*

*Former star collegiate running back Mike Holovak was a popular choice as the Patriots' second head coach. In 1963, he led the team to the AFL championship game, where they lost to a San Diego Charger team considered the best squad in AFL history.*

Charger halfback Keith Lincoln enjoyed one of the greatest all-around games in professional football history. He tallied 359 yards of total offense, which included 216 rushing yards and 123 receiving yards. He even completed a 20-yard pass. His performance stood in stark contrast to that achieved only weeks earlier in Boston, where he rushed for only 23 yards. In that game, the Chargers edged the Patriots 7–6. In the AFL championship game, they crushed the Pats 51–10.

Years later, Gino Cappelletti described the game and the Patriots' shattered dreams: "I feel we may have crashed after the Buffalo game, what with all the travel back and forth to Buffalo and then to San Diego. I feel we were at a point where we weren't able to perform like we did normally." After a slight pause, Cappelletti added, "You know, the way the Chargers played, especially on offense, it was as if they knew just what we wanted to do."

Following the game, Gillman challenged the Chicago Bears, who had won the NFL championship against the New York Giants a week earlier, to an NFL/AFL championship game. For the rest of his life, he proclaimed that his Chargers were world champions. What goes around . . .

*The 1963 Patriots beat the odds to reach the AFL championship game in San Diego only to lose by a lopsided 51–10 score before a national TV audience. It was later revealed that Chargers head coach Sid Gillman had placed spies at the Patriots' San Diego training site at a local naval base.*

guy you could ever meet. One of his weaknesses was he believed everybody . . . What he didn't think about [regarding Gillman's seemingly generous offer] is, the Chargers had several people dressed as navy guys watching practice all week long and knew what the hell we were doing."

Before a national TV audience and more than 30,000 fans at Balboa Stadium, the Chargers perfectly executed Gillman's game plan while destroying Holovak's. The Chargers raced to a 14–0 lead within minutes, foiling the Patriots' attack at every turn.

# Nance Carries the Load

*T*he image that most Patriots fans cherish of Jim Nance is that of the burly fullback carrying one or more tacklers into the end zone. For seven seasons, he was the premier power back in professional football.

At Syracuse University, Nance followed in a line of great running backs that included Jim Brown, Floyd Little, and Heisman Trophy winner Ernie Davis. Drafted by the Chicago Bears in the fourth round of the 1965 NFL Draft, Nance delayed his entry into pro football in order to compete for his second NCAA wrestling crown. By the time he'd won that title, the Bears had traded his draft rights to the New York Giants.

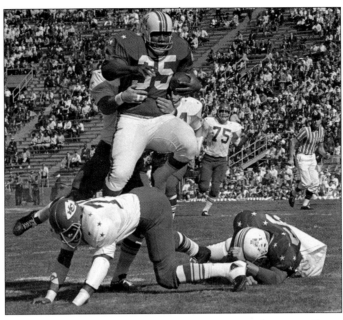

*Former Syracuse star Jim Nance was a superb athlete, excelling as an NCAA heavyweight wrestling champion and a bruising All-America fullback. His hard-charging style, displayed here in the 1968 AFL All-Star Game, made him a fan favorite in Boston.*

league, and so he signed with the Patriots.

Following a mediocre rookie season in 1965 in which Nance gained only 321 rushing yards, Patriots head coach Mike Holovak threatened to move Nance from the backfield to the trenches of the offensive line. It was then that Nance confronted a chronic eating problem that had pushed his weight from 225 to an alarming 260 pounds. For one long week, Nance endured a diet that consisted of one boiled egg at breakfast, a diet soda at lunch, and a single hamburger for dinner, followed by another diet soda before bedtime. After dropping 14 pounds, Nance never left the backfield and soon displayed the bashing style

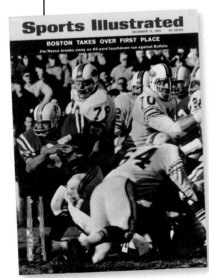

*Fullback Jim Nance was the first Patriot on a Sports Illustrated cover (December 1966), but the team suffered a mini SI cover jinx by losing their last game of the season and just missing the playoffs, finishing with an 8–4–2 record.*

After a series of additional trades, those rights finally ended up with the Cleveland Browns. Despite the fact that the Patriots had made him only their 19th-round pick, Nance was convinced he would have a better chance to star in the new

that had marked a collegiate career in which he tied the Syracuse record for career touchdowns with 13.

In 1966, Nance enjoyed a career season, scoring 11 touchdowns and leading both the AFL and NFL in rushing with 1,458 yards. Included in that total was an epic 208-yard, two-touchdown performance against the Raiders at Fenway Park. The following season, Nance maintained his relentless form, scoring seven touchdowns and again leading both leagues in rushing with 1,216 yards.

The remainder of his Patriot career was marred by injuries, and save for his performance as AFL Comeback Player of the Year in 1969, he never regained the punishing form that had earned him universal respect and the honor of being the first Patriot pictured on the cover of *Sports Illustrated.*

# Football's Nomads

From 1960 to 1971, the Patriots played their home games in seven stadiums in three states while still remaining listed in line scores as having come from Boston or New England. Few teams on any level have ever experienced as nomadic an existence.

It was fitting that Billy Sullivan brought his team to Boston University for their first three seasons. For it was here that Sullivan got his start in professional sports as the public relations wizard of the Boston Braves.

In 1963, Sullivan moved his team down Commonwealth Avenue to Fenway Park. For most of the next half-dozen seasons, the Patriots played alongside the famed Green Monster. During the Red Sox's "Impossible Dream" pennant race and World Series in 1967, the Patriots were forced to relocate for the first of their two "home" road games when they played the Chargers in San Diego. Their second distant "home" road game came in 1968, when Sullivan was sold on the idea that Alabama alumnus Joe Namath and the Jets would attract a capacity crowd to Legion Field in Birmingham, Alabama. Only 29,192 fans, however, attended the Patriots' 47–31 loss.

In 1969, the Patriots moved to Boston College's Alumni Stadium. Located in the leafy suburb of Chestnut Hill, Alumni Stadium was the site of one of the Patriots' more bizarre games. During an exhibition contest against Washington on August 16, 1970, a portion of the stands caught fire when a popcorn machine malfunctioned. As firefighters doused the flames, fans cascaded onto the field, where they chatted with players from both teams. In short time, play was resumed, and the Patriots lost to their NFL foes by a score of 45–21.

The following season the Patriots made their NFL debut at Harvard Stadium, where they won only a single game. By now the Pats had given up their dream of building a new stadium in Boston and instead had accepted the invitation of Foxboro, Massachusetts, where they built the resolutely utilitarian Schaefer Stadium.

On January 19, 2002, the team bade farewell to their old home, which had become known as Foxboro Stadium, while playing in the shadow of the superstructure of Gillette Stadium. The famed snowbound playoff game on January 19 against the Raiders remains the greatest home game in team history, and was a triumphant step by the team into a new and glorious era.

*Fenway Park served as home to the Patriots from 1963 to 1968. The home plate grandstand serves as the backdrop to this end-zone pass, which John Charles (No. 25) tipped, denying Bills receiver John Pitts a touchdown in the fourth quarter of the Patriots' 44–16 loss on December 9, 1967.*

# Home Cooking

**A**merica knows Nick Buoniconti primarily for his work as the former cohost of HBO's *Inside the NFL* and as a devoted father and philanthropist whose tireless work for the Miami Project, inspired by his son Marc's paralysis, has made him a national hero. In nearly every facet of Buoniconti's life, the former Patriot has achieved monumental success.

Buoniconti, however, who first made his name as a standout high school linebacker at Cathedral High School in Springfield, Massachusetts, had to prove himself as a football player at every successive level before his election to the Pro Football Hall of Fame in 2001.

At Notre Dame, the undersized (5′11″ and 200 pounds) linebacker played for former NFL coach Joe Kuharich and was elected captain during his senior year. Buoniconti was also an All-American, one who had his sights set on the NFL, only to be shocked when no team selected him. Instead, he was recommended to the Patriots by part-time scout and Notre Dame assistant coach Joe McArdle, who informed Patriots coach Mike Holovak of his very high opinion of Buoniconti.

*NFL scouts virtually ignored Springfield, Massachusetts, native Nick Buoniconti, who they thought was too small to make it in the pros. Chosen in the 1962 AFL Draft, the Patriots moved him from tackle to linebacker, where he soon achieved All-AFL status.*

Amazingly, Buoniconti was still available in the 13th round of the 1962 AFL Draft. The Patriots ended up paying him a mere $2,500 bonus, in addition to providing seven season tickets to his parents. It is hard to imagine a bigger bargain in franchise or NFL history.

Over the next seven seasons, he appeared in five AFL All-Star Games and helped lead the Patriots to an AFL Eastern Division title in 1963. Known as a ferocious competitor, Buoniconti was feared by teammates and opponents alike due to his full-tilt approach to games and practices. More than a few rookies got their first bitter taste of pro football on the receiving end of a Buoniconti tackle.

In 1969, the Patriots hired Clive Rush to be their head coach. He then made the first in a series of monumental blunders when he traded the future Hall of Fame linebacker to the Miami Dolphins for linebacker John "Bull" Bramlet, quarterback Kim Hammond, and a fifth-round draft choice.

In Miami, Buoniconti achieved legendary status as the leader of the famed "No Name Defense" and was a cornerstone of 1972's undefeated world champions. His stature as a hero only grew following his playing career. He has helped raise more than $100 million to date for the Miami Project as it seeks to find a cure for paralysis.

NICK BUONICONTI
BOSTON PATRIOTS  LINEBACKER

*Nick Buoniconti was a fan favorite in Boston, both as a local kid made good and as one of the most ferocious competitors in both AFL and NFL history.*

# Boston's Babe

Like most of his AFL comrades, Patriots quarterback Babe Parilli was a former collegiate All-American who had been given short shrift in limited service with the NFL. Nicknamed "Sweet Kentucky Babe" during his tenure as quarterback at the University of Kentucky under the tutelage of Paul "Bear" Bryant, Parilli was chosen as the fourth overall pick by the Packers in the 1952 NFL Draft.

His short NFL career was spent primarily with Green Bay, where he started 13 games spread over four seasons. Parilli had a short stint in 1955 with the Ottawa Rough Riders in the Canadian Football League and saw limited action with the Cleveland Browns in 1956. He joined the Oakland Raiders as their first quarterback in 1960 and was traded to the Patriots on April 4, 1961, in a blockbuster deal that sent halfback Dick Christy, fullback Alan Miller, and defensive tackle Hal Smith to Oakland for Parilli and fullback Billy Lott.

Parilli shared quarterback duties with Butch Songin in 1961 when head coach Mike Holovak instituted a new offensive system in which Parilli and Songin often alternated plays. After an injury sidelined Songin, however, Parilli stepped in to lead the Patriots to three consecutive victories to finish the season.

After Songin was traded to the New York Titans, Parilli established himself as one of Boston's most colorful athletes. Like Red Auerbach, he loved lighting victory cigars, and from 1962 to 1964, he led the Patriots to a combined record of 26–13–3. Included in this run was a road victory against the favored Bills in a tiebreaking game to decide the 1963 AFL Eastern Division title.

In six seasons with the Patriots, Parilli was a devoted disciple of the AFL's crowd-pleasing passing game. He threw for 16,747 yards and 132 touchdowns. His franchise-leading single-season touchdown record of 31, set in 1964, was finally broken by Tom Brady in 2007.

Parilli's Patriot career also included three All-Star Game appearances—in 1963, 1964, and an MVP performance in 1966. That MVP year, he threw for an astounding 2,721 yards and 20 touchdowns.

Following a dismal 3–10–1 season in 1967, the Patriots traded Parilli to the New York Jets for quarterback Mike Taliaferro. Parilli once again struck gold, winning a championship ring as Joe Namath's backup in Super Bowl III.

In 1993, Parilli was selected as a member of the fourth class of the Patriots' Hall of Fame, with the distinction of being the first quarterback chosen for that honor.

*Babe Parilli played in 94 games for the Patriots from 1961 to 1967. During that time, he was named to three AFL All-Star teams. At present, he ranks as the team's fourth all-time leading quarterback in passing yards, touchdowns, and completions.*

*Quarterback Vito "Babe" Parilli was one of a number of players cast aside by the NFL only to achieve great success in the AFL.*

# PATRIOTS PANORAMA

When he wasn't attending class at Boston's Suffolk University Law School, Nick Buoniconti was forging an All-Star career that earned him many awards. Here he holds the game ball from the Patriots' win against Buffalo in 1968.

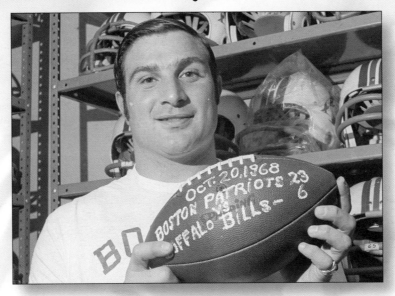

OCT. 20, 1968
BOSTON PATRIOTS 23
VS
BUFFALO BILLS- 6

HOUSTON BOSTON
OILERS / PATRIOTS
OFFICIAL PROGRAM 75¢ ASTRODOME December 14, 1969

AMERICAN FOOTBALL LEAGUE
PICTORIAL

Among the more unusual stadiums in the AFL was the Houston Astrodome. This program marks the Patriots' final game in the AFL, which was played in Houston.

The uniform of All-Star full-back Jim Nance is featured in a display at the Hall at Patriot Place, the team's museum at Gillette Stadium.

CAPPELLETTI KICKS 14 POINTS TO SPARK PATS

On December 28, 1963, Gino Cappelletti made four out of five field goals and converted two extra points to lead the Patriots to a victory against the Buffalo Bills, 26–8. The win sent the Pats into the American Football League championship game.

# From BS to New England

*I*n the wake of the Patriots' contentious exit from Boston, many in the organization were eager to jettison their Boston name. Even though many teams, such as the Detroit Lions and New York Giants, would soon leave their cities of origin, in nearly every instance their city names were left intact as a nod to both branding identity and history. No such loyalty or marketing connection existed for the Patriots. Simply put, the city had brushed them off.

Despite the best efforts of team owner Billy Sullivan to quarterback a multisport stadium complex, complete with a domed outdoor stadium for the Red Sox and Patriots and an indoor arena for the Celtics and Bruins, he was rejected at every turn by a host of Boston politicians—with the notable exception of the mayor. Following a season in which Harvard University president Nathan Pusey reluctantly allowed the Patriots the privilege of playing at Harvard Stadium, Sullivan bolted for the green pastures of Foxboro.

## FROM SCHAEFER TO SULLIVAN TO FOXBORO

Unlike most of his fellow NFL owners, Billy Sullivan was forced to build a stadium at his own expense in 1970. In response to that daunting challenge, he sought a sponsor for his facility. That sponsor was a brewery whose name was given to the stadium. Unfortunately, within months of Schaefer Stadium's opening, it quickly acquired a reputation for hosting some of the most unruly and inebriated crowds in sports.

Following the expiration of the Schaefer deal in 1983, the stadium was renamed Sullivan Stadium in honor of Billy Sullivan. In 1990, two years after Victor Kiam acquired the team, that stadium acquired a new name for a third and final time—Foxboro Stadium.

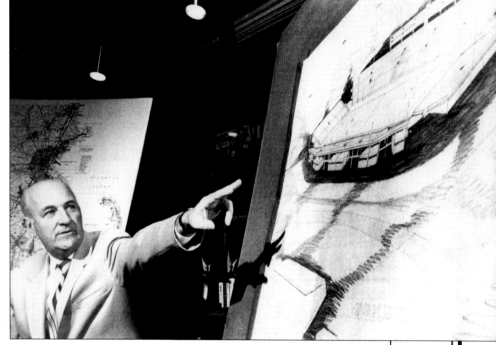

*Billy Sullivan conducts a press conference in April 1970 in which he unveils plans for Schaefer Stadium. By month's end, plans for the stadium were approved at a Foxboro town council meeting by an overwhelming margin.*

When it came time to change the team's name, it was ironic that Sullivan, a pioneer of public relations, committed a major misstep when he announced to the sports media that his team would be renamed the Bay State Patriots. The new name was a recognition of their hopes to attract fans from areas other than Boston and also a nod to their Foxboro neighbor, Bay State Raceway. In no time, sportswriters and talk show hosts tabbed the club "the BS Patriots" and commented that it was appropriate that the initials stood both for Billy Sullivan and for a "commodity" for which the charming but combative owner was renowned.

On March 22, 1971, the Patriots Board of Directors voted to formally rename the team the New England Patriots.

# A Legend Elsewhere

**B**y the time quarterback Jim Plunkett arrived at Patriots training camp in July 1971, New England fans already knew his compelling personal story. The child of blind parents, Plunkett won a football throwing contest at age 14 by tossing a ball more than 60 yards. Starring as a five-sport athlete in his native San Jose, Plunkett became a legend at Stanford University. Following his receipt of the coveted Heisman Trophy, he led Stanford to a stunning victory against Ohio State in their first Rose Bowl appearance in 18 seasons.

Success, however, proved elusive for Plunkett in New England. Although Plunkett won NFL Rookie of the Year honors in his first year with the Patriots, his second season, in 1972, saw him complete only 48 percent of his passes for eight touchdowns. Meanwhile, he was intercepted 25 times that year. His porous offensive line left him open to a bruising 36 sacks, and he paid dearly for it with less than stellar stats, as well as injuries.

Those injuries marred Plunkett's remaining four seasons with the Patriots. The team stumbled out of contention, and the bruised Plunkett continued to absorb punishment behind a shaky offensive line. By 1975, the Patriots had drafted quarterback Steve Grogan out of Kansas State and sought to trade the former All-American.

*Selected with the first overall pick in the 1971 NFL Draft, Jim Plunkett became the face and the hope of the Patriots. In five seasons with New England, Plunkett hung tough but never led the team to a winning season.*

*Jim Plunkett was the charismatic face of the franchise before injuries took their toll on the Stanford Heisman Trophy winner. Plunkett eventually found redemption with the Raiders, with whom he won two Super Bowls.*

On April 5, 1976, the Patriots sent Plunkett to the San Francisco 49ers in a block-buster deal that sent quarterback Tom Owen to New England along with the 49ers' two first-round picks in 1976 and their first- and second-round picks in 1977. Plunkett would endure more hardship in San Francisco, but he enjoyed two storybook career seasons in 1981 and 1984, when he came off the bench to lead the Raiders both to the playoffs and to upset Super Bowl victories against the Philadelphia Eagles and the Washington Redskins.

## PLUCKED FROM THE FUNNY PAGES

It isn't often that a true cultural icon plays in the NFL, but such was the case in 1972. That's when former Yale star Brian Dowling, already immortalized as the character "BD" in the comic strip *Doonesbury,* suited up for the Patriots. Cartoonist Garry Trudeau made a hero out of the former campus icon, who had never lost a game in either high school or college. Although Dowling played only three seasons in the NFL, he remains a presence on the funny pages nearly 40 years after graduating from Yale.

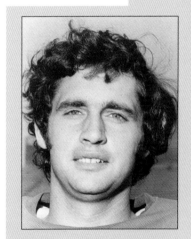

*Quarterback Brian Dowling*

# *Building a Powerhouse*

The Patriots' college drafts and free-agent signings from 1973 through 1977 are the stuff of legend. Under the direction of head coach/general manager Chuck Fairbanks and super-scout/personnel director Frank "Bucko" Kilroy, they built the core of a championship contender from the ground up.

The Patriots' strategy for the 1973 draft was to protect and support the team's most valuable asset, quarterback Jim Plun-

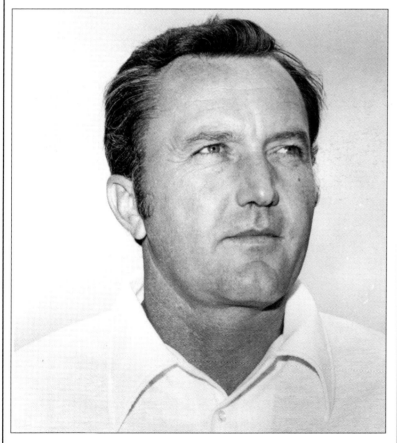

*Oklahoma coach Chuck Fairbanks was hired as the Patriots' head coach in January 1973 and presided over an era that saw the team draft such stars as John Hannah, Darryl Stingley, Steve Nelson, and Sam Cunningham. He also led the team to playoff appearances in 1976 and 1978.*

kett. In the process, they assembled what many consider the best class of draft choices in NFL history. They used their first pick, the fourth in the first round, to select future Hall of Fame guard John Hannah. They then chose future All-Pro running back Sam Cunningham with the 11th overall pick. A last-second trade of running back Carl Garrett to the Chicago Bears allowed them to select wide receiver Darryl Stingley with the 19th pick of the first round. When they reached the 14th round, they struck gold once more with the choice of defensive specialist Ray "Sugar Bear" Hamilton.

Another great signing occurred in the spring of 1973, when the Patriots inked future All-Pro tackle Leon Gray, a recent Dolphins castoff. With John Hannah, Gray later became half of the greatest weak-side offensive line in NFL history.

In 1974, the Patriots drafted future All-Pro linebacker Steve Nelson and versatile halfback Andy Johnson, but it was the Patriots' next three draft classes that came very close to the excellence of their 1973 brothers. In 1975, the team selected All-Pro tight end Russ Francis with the 16th pick of the first round, followed by linebacker Rod Shoate in the second round and fan-favorite quarterback Steve Grogan as the steal of the fifth round. The following year they parlayed the two first-round picks they had received from San Francisco in the Jim Plunkett trade to select All-Pro safety Tim Fox and center and team stalwart Pete Brock. The Pats also chose future Hall of Fame cornerback Mike Haynes with their own first pick.

The Plunkett deal delivered once again in 1977, when the Patriots nabbed All-Pro defensive back Raymond Clayborn with the 16th overall pick and running back Horace Ivory with the 44th overall pick. In addition, the Patriots' own picks were wisely used to select All-Pro wide receiver Stanley Morgan and tight end Don Hasselbeck.

Fairbanks and Kilroy are praised to this day for reaping this incredible harvest of talent for the New England Patriots.

Soccer-style kicking pioneer Charlie Gogolak was the first kicker ever chosen in the first round of the NFL draft (Redskins, 1966). He later led the Patriots in scoring in 1971.

**PATRIOTS**

**CHARLIE GOGOLAK • K**

The Patriots' Schaefer Stadium naming-rights sponsorship deal was decades ahead of its time and helped usher in an era of creative financing in pro sports, as evidenced by these stadium coasters.

**pro!**

THE OFFICIAL PUBLICATION OF THE NATIONAL FOOTBALL LEAGUE

Patriots vs. Raiders

September 19, 1971

$1. 97 CENTS
Incl. Sales Tax

Jim Plunkett And The Miracle At Foxboro

Thomas Hart Benton— Artist, Legend, Fan

May I Try Out, Coach?

Special Dedication Game Program

Jim Plunkett graced the cover of *Pro!* because he helped lead New England to a miraculous 20–6 win against the Oakland Raiders. This game in Foxboro also featured one of the worst traffic jams in modern memory.

**— LET'S BUILD A — STADIUM**

This bumper sticker was displayed on thousands of cars in the spring of 1971, while the Patriots' new home, Schaefer Stadium, was under construction in Foxboro, Massachusetts.

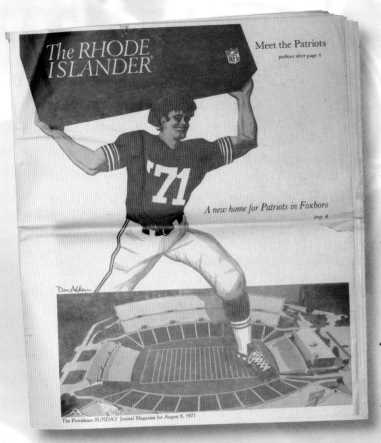

The regional appeal of the Patriots is celebrated in this 1971 supplement of *The Providence Sunday Journal*, published days before the opening of Schaefer Stadium.

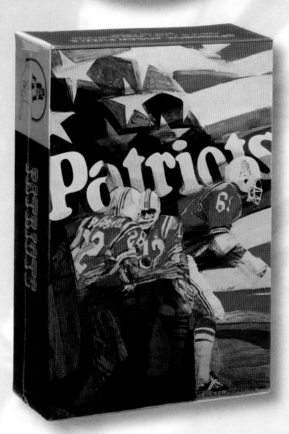

After joining the NFL in 1970, the Patriots proudly maintained their AFL identity by using the "Pat Patriot" logo for another generation. The logo is shown on this 1970s button.

Defensive back Michael Haynes combined movie-star looks with Hall of Fame talent. He was selected to the Pro Bowl six times in his seven-year Patriot career. He is shown here with the 1977 AFC Rookie of the Year trophy.

This jigsaw puzzle was one of the more colorful collectibles produced for the Patriots in the early 1970s.

# A Costly Call and Noncall

The mention of Ben Dreith still provokes deep anger in New England. On December 18, 1976, referee Ben Dreith played the role of the grinch who stole the Patriots' season when he called a controversial roughing-the-passer penalty on Patriot "Sugar Bear" Hamilton at the Oakland Coliseum. Down by four points with less than a minute to play, the Oakland Raiders faced a third down and 18 situation but then gained new life because of the penalty on Hamilton. The Patriots were assessed a 15-yard penalty, plus an additional unsportsmanlike behavior call against the irate Hamilton. The Raiders subsequently scored the winning touchdown on a one-yard keeper by quarterback Ken Stabler.

What made the Patriots' loss especially painful was the fact that the '76 team had come from nowhere to capture the hearts of New England fans. Following a disappointing 1975 campaign that saw them finish with a dismal 3–11 record, more than 10,000 fans dropped their season tickets. On Opening Day, quarterback Steve Grogan threw four interceptions in a 27–13 loss to the Colts, leaving fans with serious doubts about the team's next three games, scheduled against the dominant teams of the AFC: Miami, Pittsburgh, and Oakland.

In Foxboro, the team came alive to drub the Dolphins, 30–14, before traveling to Pittsburgh to face the defending Super Bowl champions. The dreaded "Steel Curtain" defense lived up to its name in the first half by holding the Patriots to only 22 rushing yards while maintaining a 20–9 Steeler lead into the third quarter. It was then that the '76 Patriots converted countless skeptics into believers.

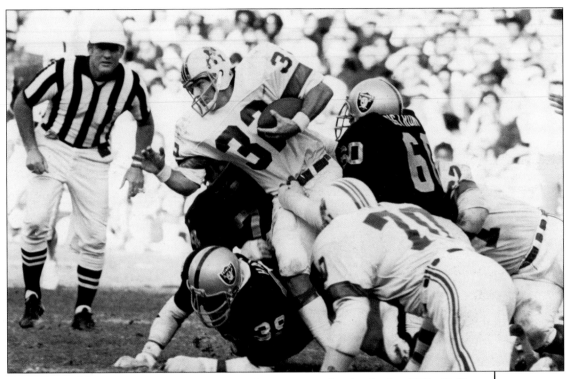

*Halfback Andy Johnson (No. 32) surges for yards against Raiders linebacker Willie Hall (No. 39) and defensive tackle Otis Sistrunk (No. 60) in the Patriots' divisional playoff game at Oakland on December 18, 1976. Their 24–21 defeat stands alongside the 2008 Super Bowl as one of the two most painful losses in franchise history.*

On a fourth-and-two call, Grogan hit tight end Russ Francis with a touchdown pass. Grogan later ran for the winning touchdown in a 30–27 victory that put New England in a tie for first place. Later that night, hundreds of fans gathered at Logan International Airport to greet their heroes.

In what fans prayed was a playoff preview, the Patriots destroyed the Raiders by a score of 48–17 before a full house in Foxboro. Oakland suffered its only loss of the season as the mobile Steve Grogan rushed for two touchdowns and passed for three more, while his counterpart Ken Stabler was sacked four times and held to just a single touchdown pass.

Not only had the Patriots survived the toughest part of their schedule, but they also went on to beat three teams that had won ten or more games the previous season. Led by their superb offensive line—fronted by John Hannah and Leon Gray—the Patriots scored an average of 26.8 points per game. Their leading rusher, Sam Cunningham, was also their second-leading receiver and a skilled blocker. Playing behind a virtual seven-man line, quarterback Steve Grogan kept opposing defenses off-kilter while scoring 12 rushing touchdowns, a single-season record for a quarterback.

After suffering a fluke 30–10 loss to the Lions, the Patriots won eight of nine games and finished in a division tie with Baltimore that gave them the wild-card slot and a playoff date in Oakland.

After a dull first half that saw the Raiders take a 10–7 lead, the Patriots capitalized on two Oakland special-teams errors to take a 21–10 lead. Oakland quarterback Ken Stabler then completed five consecutive passes on a scoring drive that left the Raiders only four points behind with just over 11 minutes to play.

New England countered with a running game designed to eat up time on the clock and move the ball. On third and inches at the Raiders' 25-yard line, however, Grogan called for a play to snap on the count of one instead of the customary short-yardage snap on the quarterback's voice. After several Patriots jumped offside, they were left with third down and a long five.

The play that resulted from this error turned out to be as controversial as the call that

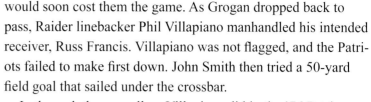

would soon cost them the game. As Grogan dropped back to pass, Raider linebacker Phil Villapiano manhandled his intended receiver, Russ Francis. Villapiano was not flagged, and the Patriots failed to make first down. John Smith then tried a 50-yard field goal that sailed under the crossbar.

In the end, the noncall on Villapiano did in the '76 Patriots as much as Dreith's infamous call. The Patriots' season was over. Still, New England fans assert that this was the best non–Super Bowl Patriots team in franchise history.

**Above:** *Oakland Raiders quarterback Ken Stabler scores the winning touchdown against the Patriots in a 1976 playoff contest that left a bitter taste in the mouths of New England players, coaches, and fans.*
**Left:** *This bobblehead doll celebrated the Patriots' new identity as the pro football team of all New England, not just Boston.*

# Hannah Paves the Way

**R**ugged. Athletic. Relentless. Ferocious. All these adjectives describe John Hannah. He was a lineman for the ages. A Mack truck with a Ferrari engine, Hannah endures as the greatest player in Patriots history. Alabama coach Bear Bryant called him "the greatest lineman I have ever coached," and *Sports Illustrated,* in a memorable cover story from August 3, 1981, proclaimed him "The Best Offensive Lineman of All Time." Almost single-handedly, Hannah elevated the status of all offensive linemen from that of rotund spear-carriers to athletes every bit as deserving of attention as the quarterbacks and running backs for whom they sacrificed their bodies.

Hannah was the product of good genes as well as great coaching. Hannah's father, Herb, was part of Alabama's offensive line and later played a single season for the New York Giants before family obligations called him back to the farm. It was Herb's example and the unfinished business of his NFL career that led sons John, David, and Charley to follow in his footsteps. All three became all-conference linemen at Alabama, with John and Charley advancing to the NFL.

John Hannah was also a talented multisport athlete, and like fellow Hall of Fame lineman Jim Parker of Baltimore, he wrestled in college while also competing for the Crimson Tide as a record-setting shot-putter and discus thrower. At his first Patriots minicamp, the 260-pound guard had

*Guard John Hannah achieved countless honors. He was named an All-Pro ten times and selected to the NFL All-Decade teams for both the '70s and '80s. Considered by many football fans to be the greatest offensive lineman ever, Hannah was named the first guard on the NFL's 75th anniversary team.*

coaches checking their stopwatches as he sprinted 40 yards in an astonishing time of 4.8 seconds.

At the height of his career in the late '70s, Hannah, at 6'2", stood smaller than many other All-Pro linemen. But his incredible balance and lateral movement made up for his lack of size. It also helped that much of his blocking was for mobile quarterback Steve Grogan. Hannah once remarked that, when blocking for Grogan, he had to make only "half a block." Fans were often treated to the sight of Hannah leading a sweep and knocking aside opponents like a uniformed bowling ball scattering pins.

*John Hannah was known for both his strength and his incredible athleticism. His trademark play was clearing the way for a sweep, leaving defenders scattered in his wake, as he does here against the Broncos.*

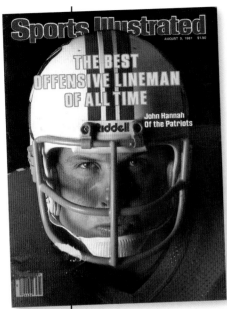

*In 1981, John Hannah's credentials as the greatest offensive lineman of all time were certified in a memorable* Sports Illustrated *cover story by Paul Zimmerman.*

In 1977, a three-game holdout with fellow lineman Leon Gray sidetracked Hannah's career. Both men wanted to renegotiate their contracts after discovering in conversations with AFC teammates at the Pro Bowl that their salaries paled in comparison with players from other teams. Both felt that Patriots ownership had used them, and so they sent letters to team president Billy Sullivan on May 1, informing the team of their intention not to play if they didn't get new deals prior to training camp.

Although both men reported to camp, they ended up sitting out the last exhibition game at home and the subsequent first three games of the regular season. During the holdout, Hannah learned that Billy Sullivan's wife, Mary, had written a letter to his mother, which included in the course of an otherwise friendly message language that questioned her son's ethics. Hannah was incensed.

Long after the dispute was settled with the assistance of the NFL Player Relations Committee, Hannah continued to harbor resentment at how management had treated him. He has only recently returned to the Patriots as a goodwill ambassador, his first formal affiliation with the team since he retired following Super Bowl XX.

In 1991, he was elected to the Pro Football Hall of Fame in his first year of eligibility. He was the first Patriot to be enshrined in Canton.

In his acceptance speech, he praised those who had helped him in his quest to be the greatest at his position: "I want to thank people like coach Chuck Fairbanks, who taught me the importance

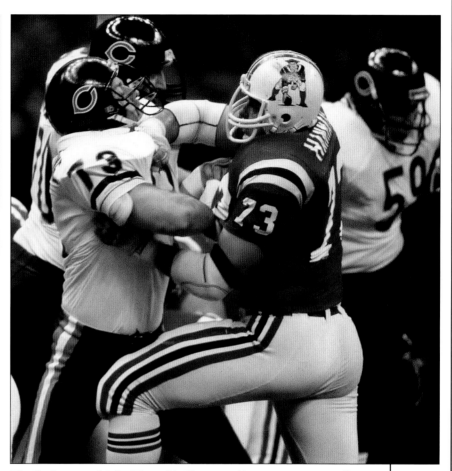

*The final game of John Hannah's illustrious Patriots career was Super Bowl XX in New Orleans. Here, Hannah battles the Bears' Mike Hartenstine in New England's humiliating 46–10 loss.*

of organization and surrounding yourself with talent so you could rely on the special gifts of others. . . . I want to thank people like Red Miller, who was my first offensive line coach in the NFL. He told me there is no better pleasure in life than to enjoy what you are doing."

After also thanking coaches Jim Ringo and Ray Berry, he remarked, "I want to thank teammates like Leon Gray, Bill Lenkaitis, Booger Bob McKay, Andy Johnson, Sam Cunningham, Steve Grogan, Steve Nelson, and Pete Brock and all the rest of the guys who were there to cover up when I missed my blocks."

# Mr. All-World

**R**uss Francis's love for the New England Patriots is so deep that he often tells the story of playing against the Miami Dolphins in Super Bowl XIX as a Patriot in the uniform of the San Francisco 49ers. Francis adds that, as the clock ticked away to the Niners' victory, his thoughts were centered less on San Francisco's triumph and more on his revenge for the many heartbreaking defeats the Patriots suffered at the hands of the Dolphins during his tenure in New England.

Francis may be the best all-around athlete to ever play for the Patriots. In high school in Hawaii, he was an all-conference quarterback, and as a baseball pitcher he even attracted an offer from the Kansas City Royals. He also averaged 20 points per game in basketball and was a record-setting javelin thrower. During the summer, he competed in local rodeos, riding bulls and bucking broncos. In his spare moments, he surfed the big waves near his home.

At the University of Oregon, he roomed with running legend Steve Prefontaine and earned second-team All-America honors in football in his junior year. During his senior year, however, he quit the football team after a dispute that arose when the head coach was fired. Despite that setback, the Patriots took a chance on Francis, who had impressed head coach Chuck Fairbanks in action against his former team, the Oklahoma Sooners.

In short time, Francis endeared himself to Patriots fans for many reasons. Not only was he movie-star handsome and an engaging public speaker, but his All-Pro skills led to his being tagged "All-World" by broadcaster Howard Cosell. In 1994, during the celebration of the Patriots' 35th anniversary, Francis was named as the team's all-time tight end by a panel of New England media.

At the time of his trade to the San Francisco 49ers following the 1981 season, Francis was the Patriots' all-time leader in receptions and touchdowns for a tight end. He remains one of the team's top ten all-time receivers in such categories as receiving yards, touchdowns, and yards per reception.

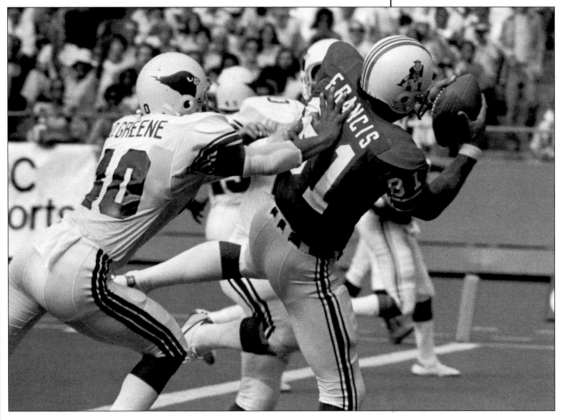

*Patriots tight end Russ Francis makes a brilliant catch against Cardinals defenders in this 1978 regular-season game.*

# The Agony and Ecstasy of the 1978 Patriots

**U**nlike the 1976 Patriots, who came from nowhere and nearly gained a Super Bowl berth, the 1978 team was expected to win. In five seasons as Patriots head coach, Chuck Fairbanks had established a solid foundation of talent, bolstered by one of the largest and best-paid coaching staffs in the business. Fans anticipated a payoff after enduring nearly 20 years of mediocrity.

On August 12, the Pats suffered a blow when star wide receiver Darryl Stingley was paralyzed in a collision with Raider defensive back Jack Tatum. The club moved quickly, acquiring receiver Harold Jackson from the Rams, and won their last two preseason games while regrouping in solemn solidarity for both their fallen teammate and one another.

Their home opener, a narrow 16–14 loss to the Washington Redskins, was followed by an easy win against the Rams in St. Louis and then another bitter home loss, 34–27, to the Baltimore Colts. Their next game was in Oakland, where

*Darryl Stingley holds the football given to him by Sam Cunningham. It's the game ball that Cunningham carried when he scored the winning touchdown against the Raiders on September 24, 1978.*

carried for the game-winning touchdown in the Patriots' last-minute 21–14 win. Their emotion-filled victory sparked a remarkable seven-game winning streak, which was part of ten victories out of their final 13 regular-season games. They ended with 11 wins, which matched the franchise high of 1976 and cast them as Super Bowl favorites.

Just as the Patriots entered the home stretch of what should have been their greatest season, it was revealed that Fairbanks was preparing to break his contract and depart to coach the University of Colorado. Fans could hardly believe it when Fairbanks was removed as coach for the team's final regular-season game, a lopsided 23–3 loss in Miami.

In the two-week buildup to their first-ever home playoff

15 players and owner Bill Sullivan visited Stingley in his hospital room. Sullivan held Stingley's hand to bid him farewell and asked him if there was anything else either he or the team could do for him. Stingley's reply was simple: "Beat Oakland."

Within four days the same group of players returned to Stingley with tearful greetings and the game ball that Sam Cunningham had

game, fans and players alike were treated to the daily soap opera of the Fairbanks/Colorado saga. Once Fairbanks was finally allowed back on the sidelines, he watched the Oilers, sparked by tight end Mike Barber's two touchdowns, destroy his demoralized team 31–14. It was Fairbanks's final NFL game and the last Patriots home playoff game for 19 years.

# The Durable Warrior

*T*he professional football career of Julius Adams was long enough that he played with such distinguished AFL alumni as Jon Morris, Houston Antwine, Don Webb, and Tom Neville. He was also an important member of the Pats' first Super Bowl team in 1986.

For 15 long years, defensive end Julius Adams slugged it out in the trenches for the Patriots. He is second only to Steve Grogan in years played for the franchise and is second in games played (206) to Bruce Armstrong (212). Drafted in 1971 out of Texas Southern University as New England's second-round pick (27th overall), Adams joined fellow rookie Jim Plunkett as an automatic starter.

Chosen to the UPI All-Rookie team, the versatile Adams spent most of his career as a defensive tackle but also saw service as a defensive end and linebacker. In 1974, he made a team-high eight sacks and was named one of the NFL's top defensive linemen by *Pro QB Magazine.* By the mid-1970s, he was the Patriots' defensive Rock of Gibraltar, helping lead the team to their 1976 and 1978 playoff appearances. A knee injury kept him out of the '78 playoff game, which is often cited as a primary reason that the talented team never made it past Earl Campbell and the Houston Oilers in the first round of the playoffs.

In 1980, with 52 tackles and a selection to the AFC Pro Bowl squad, Adams enjoyed his best season. Adams's quiet nature and superior conditioning made him one of the NFL's most consistent performers and a defender who was as apt to block a field-goal attempt as he was to make an open-field tackle. When Adams retired at the age of 39 in 1987, he was the NFL's oldest lineman and a player who had played for six of the Patriots' nine head coaches.

After he retired from the NFL, he returned to his hometown of Macon, Georgia, where he runs a farm with his wife and three sons. A hunting enthusiast, he enjoys his life away from professional football.

*Defensive end Julius Adams retired in 1987 as the Patriots' all-time leader in games played (206), a record since broken by offensive tackle Bruce Armstrong. In 2000, readers of* Patriots Football Weekly *selected Adams as a member of the franchise's All-Century team.*

# Big Dog

After the Boston Police knocked down the door to Leon Gray's apartment in Roxbury on November 11, 2001, they estimated that the former Patriot All-Pro left tackle had been dead for at least a week. Only days shy of his 50th birthday, the reclusive Gray had gone missing for two weeks before several friends contacted authorities. His death of an apparent heart attack left many friends and acquaintances pondering the life and achievements of the man known to teammates as "Big Dog."

Leon Gray was too smart to play football, but too big and talented not to play. He grew up in Olive Branch, Mississippi, where he lived alone with his grandmother in circumstances so dire he once remarked, "Grandma Jane and I were so poor and there were so many cracks and holes in the walls of our house that I could be on the inside and on the outside at the same time." In high school, Gray was an honor roll student, played lead trumpet in the band, and developed into a football player that one coach memorably described as mobile and hostile.

Gray was the first member of his immediate family to ever attend college. Although his scholarship to Jackson State was academic, it could have also been for music or athletics. On more than one occasion, Gray, clad in his dirty football uniform, grabbed his trumpet and played during halftime ceremonies. Not only did Gray start every game in four seasons, but he also gained his degree in three and a half years.

*This 1975 photo of a smiling Leon Gray shows him early in his Patriots career, before he was named to the Pro Bowl in 1976, 1978, 1979, and 1981 and before his tragic death in 2001.*

Drafted in 1973 by the Miami Dolphins, he was the last player cut at training camp and was immediately signed as a free agent by Patriots coach/general manager Chuck Fairbanks. His arrival in Foxboro was almost too good to be true; he soon joined fellow rookie John Hannah on the left side of an offensive line that legendary coach Bill Belichick, then serving as a Colts assistant, called "as good as you can get."

The 6′3″, 260-pound Gray was named to the AFC Pro Bowl squad in 1976 and 1978. It was at the 1976 Pro Bowl that he and linemate John Hannah learned from AFC teammates that their Patriot contracts were far below league standards. As a result, both men hired superagent Howard Slusher and demanded new contracts. Their three-game holdout in 1977 contributed to two Patriot losses, and only the intervention of the NFL broke the deadlock. In 1979, the Patriots broke up the pair and traded Gray to Houston for draft choices and cash.

That same year, Gray started a youth football camp with Ray Hamilton and Tony McGee. Growing up in poverty, he identified with the poor, and he wanted to help kids who endured the same disadvantages he had suffered.

After his football career, Gray should have taken advantage of his accomplishments and unique intelligence, but instead he drifted through jobs as a contractor, laborer, and beer distributor while battling depression and heart disease. In 2000, he was named to the Patriots' All-Century team. A year later, he died.

# The Last Gasp

**P**rior to the salad days of the Bill Belichick/Tom Brady era, New England's most successful stretch came in the years from 1976 to 1980. During that time, the Patriots averaged ten wins per season and delighted fans with a swashbuckling running game featuring bruising fullback Sam "Bam" Cunningham and nimble quarterback Steve Grogan. In addition to their powerful running attack, they also boasted a receiving corps led by Harold Jackson, Stanley Morgan, and "All-World" tight end Russ Francis. Entertainment value aside, however, these Patriot teams ultimately disappointed fans with only two playoff appearances, which they lost, to show for their effort.

Prior to the 1980 season, sportswriters chose the Patriots as the AFC Super Bowl favorites, and the team was even booked for three appearances on *Monday Night Football*. They started the season by proving most experts right when, after splitting their first two games, they surged with five straight wins against the Seahawks, Broncos, Jets, Dolphins, and Colts.

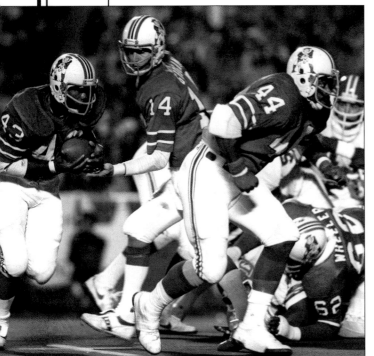

*Quarterback Steve Grogan hands the football off to running back Vagas Ferguson in a 23–14 Patriot victory against the Broncos at Schaefer Stadium. This was the first of the Patriots' three Monday night games during the 1980 season.*

*In 13 seasons with New England (1977–89), wide receiver Stanley Morgan established himself as the top receiver in franchise history, tallying more than 10,000 receiving yards and 67 touchdowns. On January 4, 1987, he made this terrific catch against the Broncos in their AFC playoff clash.*

Sporting a 6–1 record, they faced a powerful Buffalo team on October 26 at Rich Stadium with the division lead at stake. They quickly fell behind 14–3 at the half, but soon closed the gap by the end of the third quarter to 14–13. It was then that Bills halfback Joe Cribbs took the game into his own hands, scoring two touchdowns and leading Buffalo to a crushing 31–13 victory.

The balance of the season became a roller-coaster ride for the Patriots. They regained first place with a 34–21 win against the Jets before a capacity crowd at Schaefer Stadium, only to lose their grasp of the top spot after back-to-back losses to the Oilers and Rams. Brief redemption was achieved with a 47–21 rout of the Colts, and the team felt confident that their 8–4 record pointed toward the playoffs.

At Candlestick Park, the Patriots were rudely introduced to the estimable skills of the yet-to-be-great Joe Montana, who passed his 49ers into a 21–3 lead that eventually became a narrow 21–17 loss for New England. With a playoff berth at stake, the Patriots headed to Miami for a Monday night game at their house of horror, the Orange Bowl. A struggling Miami team gave them more than they could handle, and the Dolphins overcame a 13–6 deficit to snatch a 16–13 overtime win.

The loss placed the Patriots behind both the Oilers and Raiders in the hunt for what would prove to be an elusive wild-card slot. Despite the fact that the Patriots ended their season with emphatic wins over the Bills and Saints, they failed to gain a playoff spot, thus concluding the most glorious period in franchise history to date.

*This 1980 Patriots program celebrates the team's New England roots with a colorful painting that includes the team amidst both traditional architecture and resplendent fall foliage.*

## MONDAY NIGHT MAYHEM

Schaefer Stadium was the perfect name for a stadium where most fans seemed intent on having more than one beer. In fact, the Patriots' first six Monday night home games presented a series of drunken slob-fests that could only be described as equal parts *Animal House* and Hieronymus Bosch. In one particularly chilling incident, a fan was seen urinating on the shoes of a colleague who had collapsed on an exit ramp and was being given cardiac resuscitation by a crew of EMTs. The NFL soon recognized the hazards of scheduling night games at Schaefer and waited 15 seasons before turning on the night lights of Foxboro once more. Since 1994, the Kraft family has enforced strict rules regarding drinking and tailgating and has revoked many season tickets while transforming Foxboro and Gillette stadiums into family-friendly facilities.

*Patriots wide receiver Harold Jackson turns this reception into a long gainer against the Minnesota Vikings on a* Monday Night Football *telecast before a prime-time audience.*

# CHAPTER THREE

# Almost Famous

## 1981–1986

SUPER BOWL XX

AFC-NFC WORLD CHAMPIONSHIP GAME
Sunday, January 26, 1986   Kickoff 4:00 P.M.
Louisiana Superdome   $75.00

*"I tried to play like I was a football player*

*and not just a quarterback."*

### STEVE GROGAN

**Above:** *The Patriots' first Super Bowl appearance in 1986 also marked the first time a wild-card team had made it to the big game. Note the $75 price for a ticket that now sells for at least ten times that much.* **Right:** *The Patriots defense forces Dolphins quarterback Dan Marino to fumble in New England's 31–14 AFC title-game victory against Miami on January 12, 1986.*

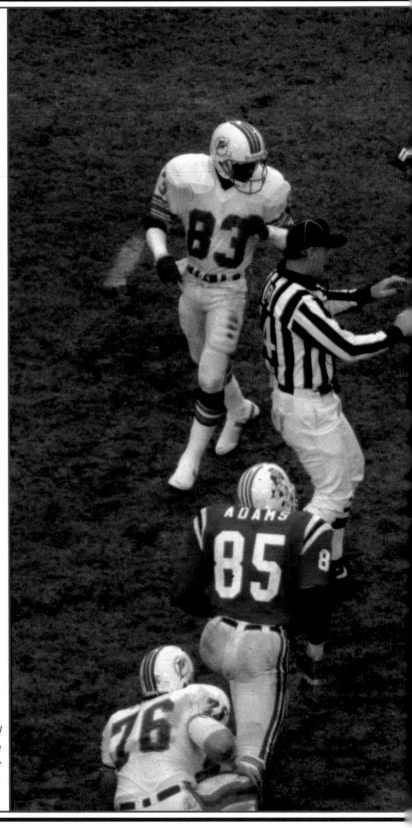

# Mr. Gamer Himself

Ask any Patriots fan over the age of 40 who their favorite player is, and most likely they will offer the name of Tom Brady, John Hannah, or Steve Grogan. The first two are future or present Hall of Fame members celebrated in the national sports media as among the best ever at their respective positions. Grogan, on the other hand, was a player whose career defied mere statistics and was best defined by football's universal yardstick—suffering. No quarterback ever endured more pain or played through a greater variety of injuries than Steve Grogan.

Grogan was so banged up that his football card could have been an X-ray. In his 16 seasons with the Patriots, the former Kansas State star might as well have been the first person to leave his body to science while still breathing. Among the injuries/operations he endured were: five knee operations, three concussions, a broken fibula, two ruptured disks in his neck, a torn tendon in his throwing elbow, a broken nonthrowing hand, and numerous cracked ribs and broken fingers. At one point, Grogan wore a neck brace to games. He even played an entire season with a ruptured disk in his neck.

Grogan played in an era when quarterbacks survived without the protection of the many rules that now allow them to operate in a virtual zone of tranquility. Not only was Grogan a talented passer, but his stylish, swashbuckling running game also helped make him one of the most entertaining performers in Patriot history. In 1976, he made news by rushing for 12 touchdowns,

*Following an injury to starting quarterback Tony Eason, fan favorite Steve Grogan entered Super Bowl XX to guide the Patriots' offense, which couldn't do much against the formidable Bears defense. New England lost the game by a tremendous margin of 46–10.*

an NFL record for a quarterback, while nearly leading his team to the Super Bowl.

Selected by Chuck Fairbanks in the fifth round of the 1975 draft, Grogan's mobile presence allowed the team to trade the talented but decidedly immobile Jim Plunkett to the San Francisco 49ers. Under Grogan's leadership, the team enjoyed a five-season run, from 1976 to 1980, during which they averaged ten wins per season with two playoff appearances. And in 1979, he was one of the last NFL quarterbacks—if not the very last—to call his own plays.

As of 2008, Grogan occupies a special place in Patriots history with a team-record 16 seasons, 26,886 passing yards (currently second to Drew Bledsoe), 182 passing touchdowns (second to Tom Brady), and an astonishing 35 rushing touchdowns (fourth all time).

"I tried to play like I was a football player," Grogan once told *The Boston Globe,* "and not just a quarterback."

*This insulated Patriots lunchbox from the 1980s is still a popular collectible.*

# End of an Era

Coming off a solid 10–6 season in 1980, the Patriots and Ron Erhardt, who was in his third full season as their head coach, were looking to improve and reach the playoffs the following year. The Pats were armed with an explosive offense, featuring quarterback Steve Grogan, receiver Stanley Morgan, and All-Pro John Hannah at guard. Added to the team's firepower was Erhardt's ability as an offense-minded coach. Such a combination seemed to promise a playoff berth.

The team started the season at home against the Baltimore Colts, a probable win for the home team. The Pats held a one-point lead going into halftime but were edged 29–28, despite a late touchdown pass from Grogan. The two teams would play again in Baltimore for the last game of the season, and again the Patriots would lose in a close game, this time 23–21. The '81 Colts got their only two wins that season against the underachieving Pats, and both teams would finish at the bottom of the league with identical 2–14 records. New England's only two wins came at home against Kansas City and Houston.

Some of the '81 team's failures could be attributed to simple bad luck. In eight of their losses they came up short by a touchdown or less, five of them by a field goal or less. But the roots of the Patriots' poor performance went much deeper than luck. Erhardt was considered to have some coaching talents, but he lacked the presence and control to be a successful head coach.

*Former offensive backfield coach Ron Erhardt took over as head coach of the Patriots in 1979, following the controversial departure of Chuck Fairbanks. In three seasons as head coach, Erhardt achieved a record of 21–27, including a disastrous 2–14 season in 1981.*

Players did not respond well to him, and they didn't enjoy playing for him. When the coach asked all the players who wanted off the team to meet with him—a late attempt to shake some life into the group—he was met by a large percentage.

Not all of the blame, however, can fall on Erhardt, a man working the wrong job. The Sullivan family, who owned the team, did not give him the power his position warranted, and they made coaching decisions that undermined his authority. Former head coach Chuck Fairbanks had been allowed to run the team as he saw fit, but the Sullivans often stepped in during Erhardt's tenure.

The following season Erhardt was out, and Ron Meyer of Southern Methodist University was named the new head coach. Meyer proved to be an even worse coach, not only losing his players' respect but unfortunately gaining their open animosity. The bitter fortunes of the 1981 team truly represented the close of a glorious era in Patriots history.

*Steve Grogan drops back to pass in the Patriots' 1981 home opener, a 29–28 loss to the Baltimore Colts. Grogan spent much of the season sharing quarterback duties with former University of Pittsburgh star Matt Cavanaugh.*

# Nelly in the Middle

For 14 seasons, Steve Nelson was the anchor of the Patriots' defense. He called signals and read offenses like a book while roaming the collision zone of the inside and middle gridiron. Don Shula once called him "the complete middle linebacker" and added, "he's got the savvy and the intensity. He's good against the pass and the run. He's very intelligent, aggressive, and emotional."

Nelson was as intense off the field as he was on it, as shown by his reaction to the Patriots' 1976 playoff loss to the Raiders at the Oakland Coliseum. Following the game, Nelson rushed to the visitors' locker room and tore the place apart. Using his helmet as a cudgel, he smashed lockers, kicked chairs, and screamed his frustration at the worst loss to date in franchise history. In the sanctuary of the locker room, Nelson's sincere expression of emotions captured the image of an intense player as beloved by fans as he was by teammates.

Nelson was selected to three Pro Bowl squads, having made more than 100 tackles in nine individual seasons, including a phenomenal 207 in 1984. Oakland coach John Madden said of Nelson, "Nelson's a hard guy, and he makes the plays. For a while they never mentioned his name when they talked about great linebackers, but we always mentioned him in scouting reports and staff meetings. We mentioned Steve Nelson's name more than he'll ever know."

Selected in the second round of the 1974 draft, Nelson enjoyed an excellent rookie season under the tutelage of Chuck Fairbanks. At the hub of the same 3-4 defensive alignment he'd played in college, Nelson almost always lined up against his opponent's strong-side guard, a position that allowed him to read offenses and recognize plays in time to communicate his observations to teammates.

Like his teammate Steve Grogan, Nelson played in pain and through injuries, including a chronically dislocated shoulder and dislocated kneecap, for most of his career. He routinely eschewed painkillers, fearing their numbing effect might lessen his ability to do his job.

In 1987, Nelson retired and noted in a press conference, "My dance card is filled. I don't want people to keep me around because of what I once contributed. I don't want my teammates to suffer. I cannot accept playing beneath the level I once did."

The Patriots retired his No. 57 after naming him to the team's Hall of Fame in 1993.

*North Dakota State's Steve Nelson was drafted in 1974 in the midst of a Patriot renaissance that saw the team nearly make it to the 1976 AFC title game. The robust linebacker remains one of the most popular figures in franchise history.*

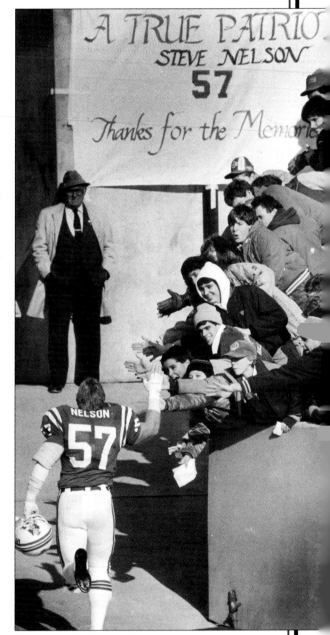

*Linebacker Steve Nelson spent his entire 14-year NFL career with the Patriots. He led the team in tackles eight times.*

# Stricken and Revitalized

At first, the NFL players' strike of 1982 seemed like a blessing to haggard Patriots fans, who had just suffered through a disastrous 2–14 record the previous season. Despite a surprising 24–13 victory against the Colts on Opening Day, the 1982 Patriots quickly reverted to form in an embarrassing 31–7 pasting at the hands of the Jets at their Schaefer Stadium home opener on the Sunday prior to the strike. But the apparent blessing ended when the NFL season resumed, with the number of regular-season games lessened from 16 to 9.

Meanwhile, the 1982 season included several makeovers for the Patriots. First, they plucked head coach Ron Meyer from Southern Methodist University, where his 1981 Mustangs had enjoyed a spectacular 10–1 season, even while serving an NCAA bowl-game probation for recruiting infractions. Known for his forceful dictatorial manner, Meyer soon ordered his players to follow a raft of seemingly arbitrary rules, such as not eating popsicles at training camp and not sitting on helmets at practice. He even alienated running back Sam Cunningham, as well as most of the team, by fining Cunningham $1,000 for his late return to the team following his mother's funeral.

*Patriot kicker John Smith connects on a game-winning field goal against the Miami Dolphins in a 1982 regular-season game.*

Part of the strike settlement from the NFL included an agreement to expand the playoff format to include eight teams from each division, which allowed the Patriots to remain in contention with a mediocre record. As the holidays approached, the Patriots clung to postseason dreams while they prepared to face the first-place Miami Dolphins in what would turn out to be their most important game in three seasons.

*While on prison work-release, stadium worker Mark Henderson gained a measure of immortality in what is now remembered as the "snowplow game." He is shown here on the tractor, clearing the way for John Smith's field-goal attempt against Miami at Schaefer Stadium.*

On December 12, while the Patriots held the Dolphins scoreless through three quarters, Foxboro was hit with a driving snowstorm. With a little more than five minutes left in the fourth quarter, the Patriots drove to the red zone. Meyer then called a timeout and ordered stadium worker Mark Henderson to use his tractor, complete with snow brush attachment, to clear a spot for kicker John Smith.

The result was a winning field goal that infuriated Miami coach Don Shula, who later commented, "That guy [Henderson] was out on the field and finished before I knew what happened. I talked with an official on our side of the field, and he said the same thing happened to him. The guy was on the field before they knew what he was doing. They will have to live with doing something like that."

Shula's revenge came less than a month later, when the Patriots fell to the Dolphins by a score of 28–13 in the snow-free confines of the Orange Bowl during the first round of the playoffs.

# PATRIOTS PANORAMA

Steve Grogan wore these turf shoes, now displayed at the Hall at Patriot Place. In 1976, he established himself as one of the NFL's greatest running quarterbacks when he rushed for a record 12 touchdowns.

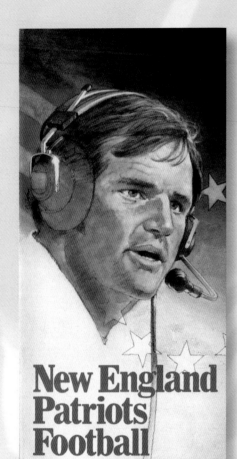

Head coach Ron Meyer, featured on this 1982 media guide, led the Patriots to a 28–13 play-off loss to the Dolphins in the strike-shortened season of 1982.

The pairing of quarterback Steve Gro-gan and wide receiver Stan-ley Morgan, as celebrated on this breakfast cereal poster, proved a major drawing card for the Patriots of the 1980s.

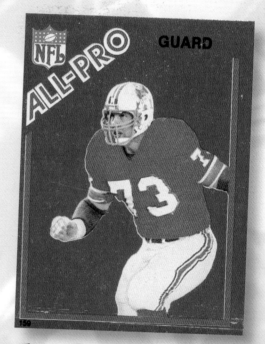

Topps paid tribute to John Hannah with this 1982 sticker card because of his outstanding career as an offensive lineman for the Patriots.

Patriots quarterback Steve Grogan poses at Sullivan Stadium with the Lamar Hunt Trophy on January 13, 1986, the day after the Patriots beat the Miami Dolphins at the Orange Bowl to clinch the AFC crown.

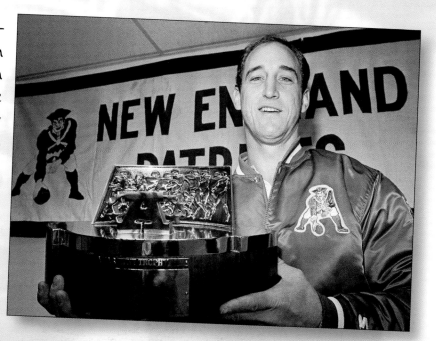

The 1981 Patriots, led by head coach Ron Erhardt, won eight fewer games than the previous season's squad. As a result, the Pats were awarded the first overall pick of the 1982 NFL Draft.

New England Patriots Football

1981 MEDIA GUIDE

Get Up for It!

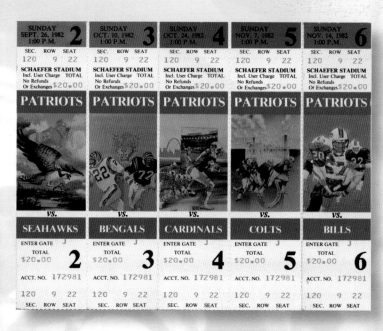

| SUNDAY SEPT. 26, 1982 1:00 P.M. **2** | SUNDAY OCT. 10, 1982 1:00 P.M. **3** | SUNDAY OCT. 24, 1982 1:00 P.M. **4** | SUNDAY NOV. 7, 1982 1:00 P.M. **5** | SUNDAY NOV. 14, 1982 1:00 P.M. **6** |
|---|---|---|---|---|
| SEC. ROW SEAT | SEC. ROW SEAT | SEC. ROW SEAT | SEC. ROW SEAT | SEC. ROW SEAT |
| 120 9 22 | 120 9 22 | 120 9 22 | 120 9 22 | 120 9 22 |
| SCHAEFER STADIUM Incl. User Charge TOTAL No Refunds Or Exchanges $20.00 | SCHAEFER STADIUM Incl. User Charge TOTAL No Refunds Or Exchanges $20.00 | SCHAEFER STADIUM Incl. User Charge TOTAL No Refunds Or Exchanges $20.00 | SCHAEFER STADIUM Incl. User Charge TOTAL No Refunds Or Exchanges $20.00 | SCHAEFER STADIUM Incl. User Charge TOTAL No Refunds Or Exchanges $20.00 |
| PATRIOTS | PATRIOTS | PATRIOTS | PATRIOTS | PATRIOTS |
| vs. | vs. | vs. | vs. | vs. |
| SEAHAWKS | BENGALS | CARDINALS | COLTS | BILLS |
| ENTER GATE J | ENTER GATE J | ENTER GATE J | ENTER GATE J | ENTER GATE J |
| TOTAL $20.00 **2** | TOTAL $20.00 **3** | TOTAL $20.00 **4** | TOTAL $20.00 **5** | TOTAL $20.00 **6** |
| ACCT. NO. 172981 | ACCT. NO. 172981 | ACCT. NO. 172981 | ACCT. NO. 172981 | ACCT. NO. 172981 |
| 120 9 22 | 120 9 22 | 120 9 22 | 120 9 22 | 120 9 22 |
| SEC. ROW SEAT | SEC. ROW SEAT | SEC. ROW SEAT | SEC. ROW SEAT | SEC. ROW SEAT |

The *Patriots Report* was a popular New England sports newspaper that premiered in September 1981. This cover features quarterback Steve Grogan.

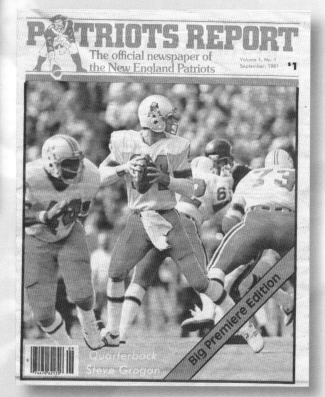

PATRIOTS REPORT

The official newspaper of the New England Patriots

Volume 1, No. 1 September, 1981 $1

Big Premiere Edition

Quarterback Steve Grogan

Unfortunately for Patriots management, there were countless unused tickets in 1982. Crowds barely filled half the seats at Schaefer Stadium for games against traditional rivals such as the Dolphins and Bills.

# The British Are Coming

John Smith's story could serve as the basis for the perfect Hugh Grant script. Erudite Englishman arrives in America, college degree in hand, eager to pursue his dream of teaching and coaching soccer, and instead ends up making a living in a sport he had never watched, much less played.

Smith's improbable journey to the National Football League started in 1972, when the 22-year-old graduate of Southampton University came to the United States to coach soccer at Camp America in Lenox, Massachusetts, while seeking steady employment as a teacher. It was here that he impressed a camper who happened to be the son of Cleveland Browns vice president Bob Griese (not the quarterback). This led the former Queens Park Rangers soccer trainee to a series of kicking tryouts that never panned out, and before long Smith returned to England.

## THE LEGEND OF SUPERFOOT

Among the more legendary stunts of the Boston sports radio talk-show team of Mark Witkin, Jim McCarthy, and Eddie Andelman, known as *The Sports Huddle,* was their 1971 international manhunt for a field-goal kicker for the Patriots. Tabbed "Search for Superfoot," the trio's project

ultimately attracted 1,600 Britons, lured by a $1,000 prize and a chance to kick in the NFL. Mike Walker, a 21-year-old bricklayer from Camforth, Lancashire, kicked two 55-yard field goals to win the contest. He ultimately played for part of the 1972 season before losing the kicking job to veteran Charlie Gogolak.

*Mike Walker earned a job with the Pats after winning a kicking contest in Oxford, England.*

*In ten seasons with the Patriots, from 1974 to 1983, John Smith led the team in scoring eight times. He is pictured here kicking one of many field goals at Foxboro Stadium.*

In 1973, however, Smith received a call from Patriots executive Peter Hadhazy inviting him to a four-day free-agent tryout. On the eve of his wedding, Smith figured he'd enjoy an expenses-paid vacation overseas, never figuring his kicking skills would gain him a lucrative career.

Despite making an impressive showing in training camp, Smith was traded in a paper deal with the Steelers. After Pittsburgh cut Smith, he returned to Foxboro, where the Patriots re-signed him. He spent the rest of the 1973 season kicking for the minor-league New England Colonials and studying his craft while attending college games across New England on Saturday afternoons.

In 1974, he made the most of his kicking apprenticeship and won a job he'd keep for ten seasons. On his retirement following the 1983 season, Smith stood second to Gino Cappelletti in Patriots all-time scoring with 692 points; he currently stands in third place behind Cappelletti and Adam Vinatieri.

# On the Road

Fresh from their victory against the Bengals in the raucous final regular-season game at Sullivan Stadium in 1985, the Patriots packed their bags with more than just an extra pair of socks in anticipation of a month-long journey to the Super Bowl. The fact that no wild-card team had ever reached the title game mattered little to these road warriors.

On December 28, the Patriots faced a Jets team that matched their 11–5 record and was considered the best Jets squad since the salad days of Joe Namath. Led by quarterback Ken O'Brien and a defensive line featuring Mark Gastineau and Joe Klecko, the Jets provided a stiff challenge. Not only had the Patriots never won a single playoff game in their 25-year history, but they had also lost in overtime to the Jets by a score of 16–13 on the road just a month earlier.

*Patriot running back Craig James slices between New York Jets defensive end Mark Gastineau (No. 99) and linebacker Lance Mehl (No. 56) during the Patriots' 26–14 wild-card playoff victory at Giants Stadium on December 28, 1985.*

Led by quarterback Tony Eason, the Patriots played a solid ground game and led 3–0 after the first quarter. They stretched their lead to 13–7 after kicker Tony Franklin nailed a 41-yard field goal and Stanley Morgan raced 36 yards with a touchdown reception. The Patriots prevailed in a 26–14 win, leaving them two wins away from the Super Bowl.

Their next game was against their most hated rivals, the Los Angeles Raiders. Not only had the Raiders barely beaten New England in a controversial 1976 divisional playoff game, but the Raiders were also the team of Jack Tatum, whose paralyzing hit on Patriot wide receiver Darryl Stingley seemed to capture the reckless outlaw spirit of owner Al Davis's men in silver and black.

On a balmy afternoon at the Los Angeles Coliseum, the Patriots finally exacted revenge for years of hurt and disappointment, beating the Raiders 27–20 courtesy of six turnovers, including a fumble recovery by Patriot safety Jim Bowman for the winning touchdown.

## GM SULLIVAN TAKES A HIT

During the Patriots' 1985 playoff game against the Raiders, Patriots general manager Patrick Sullivan chose to watch the game from the sidelines adjacent to the Patriot bench. As one of the Patriot assistant coaches yelled insults at Raider defenders, word spread that it was actually Sullivan doing the honors. At the end of the game, Raider defensive end Howie Long exchanged verbal blows with Sullivan, who followed him toward the Raider locker room. It was here that Sullivan took on several more Raiders, and in the resulting scuffle, Raider linebacker Matt Millen whacked Sullivan on the head with his helmet. The eight stitches in Sullivan's scalp remain a badge of honor from an afternoon when football's bullies from Oakland went far overboard.

*Matt Millen (No. 55) of the Los Angeles Raiders clobbers the head of Patriots general manager Patrick Sullivan. The ugly incident followed the Patriots' divisional playoff victory at the Los Angeles Coliseum on January 5, 1986.*

# Patriots Squish the Fish

*I*t was the slogan that captured the spirit of the 1985 Patriots playoff run and also sold several thousand T-shirts. To this day, one can spot fans at Gillette Stadium clad in one of the many variations of the "Squish the Fish" T-shirts that symbolized the Patriots' improbable Super Bowl quest. Many of them depict the manic cartoon figure of Pat Patriot strangling a hapless dolphin.

The Patriots' AFC championship win against the Miami Dolphins on January 12, 1986, generated as much hype as any Red Sox, Bruins, or Celtics victory. Like the "Impossible Dream" Red Sox of 1967, the magnitude of the Patriots' journey could only be fully appreciated in the context of both their checkered past and the problematic saga of pro football in New England.

Up until this time, the region's sole football champion was the 1928 NFL Providence Steam Rollers. The Boston Redskins should have been the next New England team to secure a championship, but in 1936, owner George Preston Marshall sent his team to New York's Polo Grounds.

*Running back Robert Weathers races for much of the 87 yards he gained in the Patriots' 31–14 AFC championship win against the Dolphins at the Orange Bowl. He also grabbed a two-yard touchdown pass from Tony Eason, which gave New England a 24–7 lead in the third quarter.*

*Barefooted Patriots place-kicker Tony Franklin boots a 23-yard field goal in the Patriots' AFC championship win against Miami.*

In 1937, this same team won their first NFL championship as the Washington Redskins.

Led by halfback Craig James and linebacker Steve Nelson, the Patriots went to Miami confident of victory. Nelson would later remark to sportswriter Jim Donaldson, "When we took the field, we knew we were the better team. We'd beaten them in New England [17–13] in early November, and they'd beaten us in Miami [30–27] in a sloppy game on a Monday night in week 15."

The Patriots' game plan was simple: Run the ball down their throats, kill the clock, and keep the ball away from Miami All-Pro quarterback Dan Marino and his killer receiving corps of Mark Clayton, Mark Duper, and Nat Moore. Patriot quarterback Tony Eason spent most of the game handing off to Craig James, who gained 105 yards on 22 carries, as well as to fullback Robert Weathers, who chipped in with 87 yards, and to receiver and running back Tony Collins, who not only rushed for 61 yards but also caught the go-ahead touchdown. When Eason did throw on the muddy field, he completed 10 of 12 passes for 71 yards, as well as three short-range touchdowns.

The Patriots not only decisively beat the defending AFC champions 31–14, but they also exorcised the ghosts that had haunted their franchise. They had won their first AFC championship, which would allow them to play in their first Super Bowl. Owner Billy Sullivan wiped away tears and then hugged each player as they left the playing field.

# Leader of the Pats

Quiet, reserved, studious, persistent, and prepared. All these words describe the personality of former Patriot head coach Raymond Berry. As a player, he was one of the NFL's greatest wide receivers and was the primary target of quarterback extraordinaire Johnny Unitas in the glory days of the Baltimore Colts. In the unforgettable NFL championship game of 1958, Berry caught 12 passes for 194 yards in the Colts' dramatic 23–17 overtime victory against the New York Giants.

Following his Hall of Fame playing career, Berry served as the Patriots' assistant coach for receivers under Chuck Fairbanks and Ron Erhardt before being fired with the Erhardt regime following the 1981 season. When Patriots general manager Pat Sullivan approached him about the head coaching position in 1984, he had already worked outside football for nearly three years and was hesitant to take a job he knew would eventually end with his firing.

*Patriots head coach Raymond Berry clutches the game ball while being carried off the field following his team's 31–14 win against the Miami Dolphins in the 1985 AFC championship game.*

Shortly after being hired, he said, "My job is to make something good out of a bad situation." Fans remained skeptical after the team dropped three of their first five games, but they soon jumped on the bandwagon when the Patriots ripped through a six-game winning streak that included victories against the playoff-bound Jets and Dolphins. While Berry repeatedly told his team to relax and stay focused, veteran quarterback Steve Grogan, who had replaced the injured Tony Eason during the streak, came in to inspire the team.

Down the stretch, Berry's team won three of their last four games to grab the wild-card slot that resulted in one of the most memorable months in New England sports history. He led his team to an unprecedented three consecutive road playoff wins and a trip to Super Bowl XX in New Orleans.

Berry remained as head coach for another two seasons, during which he led the team to a regular-season

Not only was the understated Raymond Berry a welcome relief from his overbearing predecessor, Ron Meyer, but his résumé commanded instant respect from his team. As a former player, Berry knew that his greatest challenge was to extract maximum performance from his squad while keeping them healthy and motivated.

division crown in 1986. But after a playoff loss in Denver to end the '86 season, the Pats disappointed their fans the following year with a mediocre 8–7 record in a strike-shortened season.

His .554 winning percentage ranks second to Bill Belichick on the Patriots' all-time coaching roster, and only he and Belichick have more playoff wins than losses as a Pats head coach.

# Mauled at Super Bowl XX

The memories of football fans in New England are selective when it comes to the Patriots' first Super Bowl. Many remember the Bears' tacky music video for "The Super Bowl Shuffle" as being better than the Patriots' lame "Berry the Bears" fight song. The lucky few will indicate they were happy to stroll down Bourbon Street, trade verbal barbs with Chicagoans, and take in the joys of the "Big Easy" before the "Big Game." Others will tell of Super Bowl parties with friends and relatives that brought generations together in celebration of a never-say-die team. And then there are those who still complain that Grogan should have started at quarterback and that the Bears were given an unfair advantage by the media hype surrounding their powerhouse team.

Many Patriots fans, however, were simply happy their team had made it to the Superdome.

Fans hoped for the best when the Patriots jumped out to a quick three-point lead, thanks to Tony Franklin's 36-yard field goal. During the two hours that followed, however, the Chicago Bears simply knocked the living daylights out of the Patriots. No game plan or individual heroics could have rescued the Pats on a day when the Bears showed that they were one of the greatest teams of all time.

The Bears scored in every possible way, icing the cake with a fourth-quarter safety on an end-zone tackle of Steve Grogan as the game came to a close. In between, Bears kicker Kevin Butler booted three field goals, quarterback Jim McMahon scored

*The Patriots' first Super Bowl, in 1986, came during a year when New England also celebrated the Boston Celtics' 16th world championship and the Red Sox's epic World Series battle with the New York Mets.*

*Four Patriot defenders tackle Bears running back Walter Payton during Super Bowl XX. The Patriots held the Hall of Famer to 61 rushing yards, but Chicago nevertheless crushed New England in a 46–10 rout.*

twice on keepers, fullback Matt Suhey charged 11 yards for a touchdown, defensive back Reggie Philips scored on a 28-yard interception return, and 308-pound rookie defensive lineman William "Refrigerator" Perry scored the Bears' final touchdown on an in-your-face one-yard plunge, all contributing to a 46–10 rout. The Bears did everything short of petitioning the NFL Rules Committee at halftime to allow them to score via dropkick or a Canadian-style rouge.

Even diehard Bears fans winced as head coach Mike Ditka embarrassed the Patriots when he denied All-Pro halfback Walter Payton the chance to score what could have been his sole Super Bowl touchdown. Having Perry run into the end zone instead of

Payton remains one of the tackiest moves in sports history—a sour footnote to one of the most overpowering performances in American pro team sports.

In a conversation with Paul Zimmerman of *Sports Illustrated*, Patriot right guard Ron Wooten later remarked, "We just floundered around. The pressure got to us. If I could do one thing differently, I'd like to go out and challenge the Bears with what got us there, running the ball, but we didn't. Probably we shouldn't have. The Bears are just better than we are right now. I'm not embarrassed. I'm humiliated."

If Super Bowl XX had been a boxing match, the referee would have called a TKO by the second round. Ditka's Chicago Bears were nothing short of a living anthology of all the great Bear teams of the past, with Mike Singletary playing the role of Dick Butkus, Jim McMahon imitating Hall of Fame quarterback Sid Luckman, running back Walter Payton playing himself, and Ditka channeling the late Papa Bear, George Halas. Surely these were a second version of the famed "Monsters of the Midway."

Upon their return to Boston, the Super Bowl Patriots were humbled yet again by a story in *The Boston Globe* alleging

*Wide receiver Irving Fryar celebrates the Patriots' lone touchdown in their Super Bowl loss to the Chicago Bears in New Orleans.*

rampant drug use by six players: Irving Fryar, Stephen Starring, Ken Sims, Raymond Clayborn, Tony Collins, and Roland James. Following the story's publication, it was learned that the test results came from previous seasons and that coach Raymond Berry had helped each player get clean prior to their Super Bowl campaign.

Such is the checkered tale of a team that should be remembered for their glorious and unprecedented journey to New Orleans—rather than their humiliating mauling by the mighty Bears.

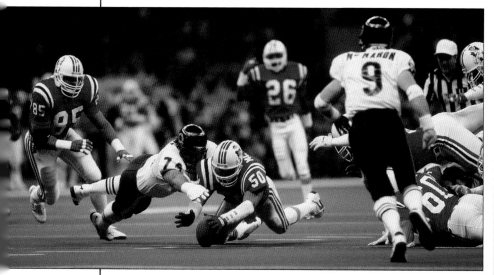

*Patriot Larry McGrew (No. 50) dives for a loose ball alongside Bear Jim Covert (No. 74) on the Superdome turf during Super Bowl XX.*

*This colorful 1986 bumper sticker, which was sold in Boston and Chicago, was effective in promoting Super Bowl XX.*

This segment of a goal-post was torn from the turf of Sullivan Stadium on December 22, 1985, after the Patriots defeated the Bengals to clinch a wild-card playoff berth.

Factories worked overtime in early 1986 to produce these buttons as Patriots fans finally had a reason to celebrate.

The day after the Patriots knocked off the Dolphins to win the AFC, head coach Raymond Berry was shown on the front page of the January 13, 1986, issue of *The Boston Globe*.

Following the Patriots' victory against the Dolphins in the 1985 AFC title game, the team's rallying cry went from "Squish the Fish" to "Berry the Bears," in honor of Patriots head coach Raymond Berry.

# Huckster's Paradise

Victor Kiam was already a familiar figure to Patriots fans when he and minority owner Fran Murray purchased the team from the Sullivan family on July 28, 1988. As owner of the Remington Corporation, his ubiquitous television commercials, which featured an enthused Kiam exclaiming, "I liked [the electric shaver] so much, I bought the company," were a staple on network sports broadcasts.

In the beginning, fans were hopeful that the egocentric pitchman might bring a competitive fire, reminiscent of George Steinbrenner, along with his unique business savvy, one that had seen Kiam parlay an initial investment of a half-million dollars into profits of nearly $700 million at Remington. Kiam, whose local roots included degrees from Phillips Andover, Yale, and Harvard Business School, was recognized as both a workaholic and a man capable of making lemonade from the bushel of lemons he'd just purchased in Foxboro.

Instead, fans were treated to a soap opera of epic proportions, featuring the all-too-familiar scenario of an owner whose ego allowed him to surmise that his Wall Street acumen was easily transferred to football.

Remington razor magnate Victor Kiam, owner of the Patriots from 1988 to 1992, addresses the sports media on December 20, 1990. That season the Patriots were a miserable 1–15.

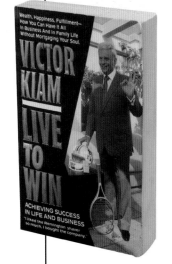

*Although Victor Kiam was a winner in his business career, the best-selling author/pitchman's foray into pro football proved to be disastrous.*

When businessman Victor Kiam remarked, "You can hype a questionable product for a little while, but you'll never build an enduring business," he could well have been describing his rocky tenure as owner of the Patriots. In four seasons (1988–91), his team managed to win only 21 games while racking up 43 losses. Not only did his team lose with regularity, but in 1990, the Patriots also disgraced themselves during a locker room incident in which several players exposed themselves to *Boston Herald* reporter Lisa Olson. The resulting scandal not only forced Kiam to sell his interest in the team, but it nearly cost New England the Patriots.

In a short time, Kiam went from celebrated tycoon to the hapless team owner parodied by comedian Phil Hartman in a memorable skit on *Saturday Night Live*. Copies of his book *Live to Win: Achieving Success in Life and Business* eventually found their way to the remainder pile of local bookstores, where they sold for a dollar. More than a few Patriots fans received copies as gag gifts from friends who supported the Giants or Jets.

Kiam once said, "Entrepreneurs are risk takers, willing to roll the dice with their money or reputations on the line in support of an idea or enterprise. They willingly assume responsibility for success or failure of a venture and are answerable for all its facets."

On May 11, 1992, Victor Kiam was held responsible for the debacle of the New England Patriots. His controlling interest in the team was sold to Anheuser-Busch heir James Busch Orthwein.

# Irving Fryar, the "Human Headline"

Irving Fryar was one of the best athletes to play for the Patriots. Not only was he clocked at 4.25 seconds in the 40-yard dash, but he also had an incredible 42-inch vertical leap. In 1984, when the Patriots drafted him, Fryar became the first wide receiver ever chosen with the first overall pick in the NFL draft.

For all his talent, however, Fryar arrived in Foxboro with a lot of baggage. Rumor had it that he was high on cocaine the night before he played for the Nebraska Cornhuskers against Miami in the 1984 Orange Bowl. Sportswriter and CBS sideline reporter Armen Keteyian would later allege that Fryar deliberately dropped a pass in the game in an attempt to influence the score.

*Boston Herald* sportswriter Michael Felger called him "the human headline," and with good reason. Thumb through Fryar's considerable Patriots clip file, and you'll see far more stories on his off-the-field exploits than those detailing his Pro Bowl talents.

Among the more noteworthy stories was one that detailed the injury that kept him out of the 1985 AFC title game. Fryar claimed that he had cut himself while working in his kitchen several nights before the game; only later was it revealed that his wife, Jacqui, had sliced the star receiver's hand with a kitchen knife wielded during a heated domestic argument.

In 1987, Fryar caused a ruckus on the NFL player picket line when he tossed eggs at replacement players. He also jumped on the bumper of assistant coach Bobby Grier's car as Grier transported replacement players to the practice field.

Later that season he claimed to have been robbed at gunpoint at a jewelry store in downtown Boston, despite the fact that neither he nor the jeweler filed a police report. In 1988, New Jersey police pulled

*Wide receiver Irving Fryar stretches to make a game-winning catch of Tony Eason's Hail Mary pass with no time remaining in the Patriots' come-from-behind 30–28 win against the Los Angeles Rams on November 16, 1986.*

*This Hi-Pro card celebrates Irving Fryar's 1989 season, in which he caught 29 passes.*

him over for a suspended license and discovered a loaded rifle and hollow-point bullets in his car. He was nearly killed in a 1990 incident at a bar in Providence, Rhode Island, when he tried to defend teammate and fellow wide receiver Hart Lee Dykes with a handgun before being knocked unconscious with a baseball bat.

Finally, on April Fools' Day in 1993, the Patriots decided they'd had enough of Fryar. Coach Bill Parcells traded his troubled star to Miami for a second-round pick in that year's draft and a fourth-round pick in the 1994 draft.

# Eleven Years of Intimidation

In 2008, Andre Tippett became only the second Patriot to play his entire career with New England while earning a place in the Pro Football Hall of Fame in Canton, Ohio.

In 11 seasons with the Patriots (1982–88, 1990–93), Tippett was named to five consecutive Pro Bowls, recorded franchise-leading career totals of 100 sacks and 19 recovered fumbles, and was named the NFL Players Association's top linebacker in 1985, 1986, and 1987, each year ahead of New York Giants legend and fellow Hall of Fame member Lawrence Taylor.

During his days as head coach of the Cleveland Browns, Bill Belichick once remarked of Tippett: "We'd watch him play and talk to our players about 'See how he's doing that? That's the way we want you to do it.' He was one who was every bit as dominating of a player in his time and in his game."

Tippett, along with Lawrence Taylor, redefined the position of outside linebacker. He excelled in the hand-to-hand combat of pass rushing, using the skills he had learned while earning a black belt in karate. Teammate Don Hasselbeck hated to practice against him and claimed his worst football injuries came as the result of his weekly skirmishes with Tippett.

Unlike Taylor—who starred for Super Bowl champions and perennial contenders—Tippett established his reputation far from the media spotlight. The Pats enjoyed only six winning seasons and three playoff appearances during his 11 years in Foxboro.

When Patriots owner Robert Kraft introduced Tippett at his Hall of Fame induction ceremony, he said, "Andre possessed the perfect combination of strength, speed, and athleticism. In his prime, Andre was probably the most intimidating player in the game."

Kraft also extolled Tippett's character when he said, "It was in 1989, at Mass General Hospital, where...I was visiting my son David, who had just suffered a very serious knee injury that had ended his wrestling season.... Andre, who had just suffered a season-ending injury, insisted on visiting my son to cheer him up. To think that this man, who was so ferocious and intimidating on the field could be so gracious and thoughtful off of it, to me these are the traits that make Andre so special."

*Starting Lineup selected only the best NFL players, and linebacker Andre Tippett was one of them in 1989.*

*Tippett, shown here in action against the Broncos in 1987, was considered the equal of fellow linebacker Lawrence Taylor during his 11 seasons with the Patriots. Tippett was elected to the Pro Football Hall of Fame in 2008.*

In Tippett's own remarks at his induction ceremony, he made special mention of his extended Patriot family, which included former player-development specialist Dick Steinberg, general manager Pat Sullivan, and former coach Raymond Berry, of whom he said, "Raymond Berry…taught me the value of preparation and understanding the business is winning football games. Under coach Berry we became the first team to take the organization to the Super Bowl. The single greatest moment of my career."

While looking at former teammate and fellow Hall of Fame member John Hannah, Tippett said, "To the veterans who helped show the way, John Hannah and Mike Haynes,…and to the young guys who challenged me as I became the old man on the team, thank you guys." In closing, he paid tribute to Patriots fans while observing, "You are our backbone. You are why we do what we do."

**Above:** *Tippett levels New York Jets quarterback Ken O'Brien in the Patriots' first playoff win of the magical 1985 season. Such hits helped establish Tippett's reputation as one of the most feared linebackers in the NFL.*
**Left:** *This 1989 Starting Lineup figure of Tippett is a favorite of New England collectors.*

*Hall of Fame linebacker Andre Tippett (No. 56) takes a break with teammate Corwin Brown during action against the Buffalo Bills at Foxboro Stadium in 1993.*

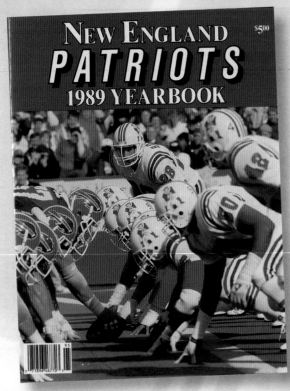

The 1989 Patriots finished with a disappointing 5-11 record, prompting the firing of head coach Raymond Berry on February 26, 1990.

Boston fans placed punter Rich Camarillo on the franchise's All-Century team in 2000. The back of this 1988 Topps card notes that he kicked the longest AFC punt of the 1987 season (73 yards).

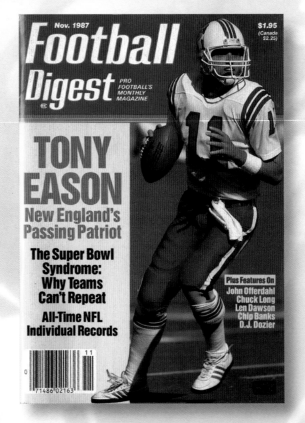

This 1989 book provides practical guidelines for entrepreneurs. To Patriots fans, however, Victor Kiam's failures as Patriots owner overshadowed his success as an entrepreneur.

Tony Eason is shown on the cover of *Football Digest*. He played with the Patriots for seven seasons and helped lead New England to Super Bowl XX.

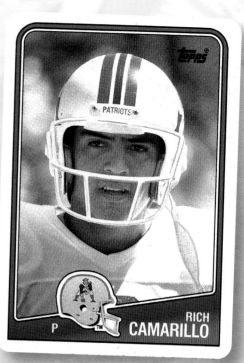

Although the Victory Tour story was secondary to the news about the Sullivan family's sale of the Patriots in this April 1, 1988, issue of *The Boston Globe*, it was a major reason why the family was forced to sell the team.

As described on the back of this Score card, running back John Stephens gained 1,168 rushing yards in 1988, thus capturing NFL Rookie of the Year honors.

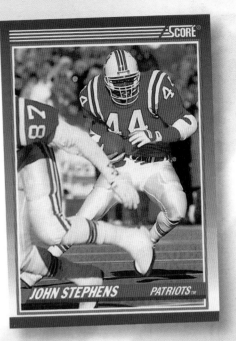

Andre Tippett poses with his Pro Football Hall of Fame bust during halftime ceremonies at a game between the Patriots and Broncos.

In 1988, the Patriots' quarterback chores were split between the pictured Steve Grogan (No. 14) and Heisman Trophy-winning local hero Doug Flutie.

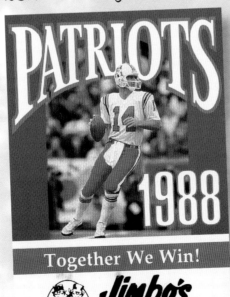

All-Pro wide receiver Stanley Morgan graces the cover of this 1987 Patriots fact book. The team finished with a record of 8-7 in the strike-shortened season to tie for second in the AFC East.

# A Dark Page in Patriot History

**O**n September 17, 1990, the Patriot franchise disgraced itself with the unimaginable actions of three players who sexually harassed *Boston Herald* reporter Lisa Olson. The incident began when she tried to interview cornerback Maurice Hurst on the day after what turned out to be the Patriots' only victory of the season.

Tight end Zeke Mowatt was a player vocal in his opposition to the presence of female reporters in the locker room. He was the first to accost the 26-year-old reporter. In a report filed by former Watergate attorney Philip Heymann, who was acting as a special counsel for NFL commissioner Paul Tagliabue, Mowatt allegedly made crude comments about Olson to tackle Bruce Armstrong. Unclothed, Mowatt proceeded to confront Olson and mercilessly taunt her.

Running back Robert Perryman also taunted the helpless reporter with his own physical gestures. Several other Patriots, including wide receiver Michael Timpson, joined the ugly scene.

*Sports reporter Lisa Olson interviews Patriots wide receiver Irving Fryar at Sullivan Stadium in 1990.*

After reporting the incident to her editors at the *Boston Herald,* the newspaper asked for a private meeting with Patriot executives and requested both an apology and a chance to meet with the players in question. Olson didn't want the story to break, but before the team took any action, the story appeared in *The Boston Globe.*

Not only did all hell break loose, but the situation took a turn for the worse when Olson soon became the target of fan attacks. First, Patriots owner Victor Kiam called her an ugly name during a conversation overheard in the visitors' locker room at Cincinnati's Riverfront Stadium just

*NFL commissioner Paul Tagliabue eventually launched an investigation of the Olson incident that resulted in player fines.*

six days after the incident. Kiam only made things worse when he told the *Boston Herald* that his remarks were misinterpreted, adding, "I can't disagree with the players' actions. Your paper is asking for trouble by sending a female reporter to cover the team."

Olson soon became a virtual punching bag for fans. Not only was the front of her apartment spray-painted with a pejorative, but vandals also broke into her apartment and ransacked it. They scrawled "Leave Boston or die" on her walls. Fans at Foxboro Stadium also vilified her, chanting her name during games.

Her editors quickly reassigned her to cover the Celtics and later the Bruins, but she still was subjected to the indignity of having drinks and food thrown at her. Olson even suffered a punch from one disturbed fan.

After NFL commissioner Paul Tagliabue deemed the Patriots' internal investigation—which included fining Mowatt just $2,000 of his $650,000 salary—a joke, the league conducted its own probe into the incident. The lengthy, highly publicized investigation not only tore the team apart as players ratted on one another, but several executives, including head coach Rod Rust and general manager Patrick Sullivan, were also made scapegoats and fired in the aftermath of the worst incident in franchise history.

In the wake of the mess, Sullivan would later accuse Tagliabue of destroying the Patriots while playing up to *Boston Herald* owner Rupert Murdoch, whom he was then courting for a possible NFL television deal. Ultimately, Mowatt was fined $12,500, Perryman and Timpson $5,000 apiece, and the team $50,000, while Olson decided to move

*Lisa Olson not only covered the New England Patriots while she worked for the* Boston Herald, *but she also reported on the Red Sox, Celtics, and Bruins.*

to Sydney, Australia, where she worked in the sports departments of *The Daily Telegraph* and *The Sydney Morning Herald.*

Several weeks after paying the NFL fine, Kiam rekindled the controversy by making Olson the butt of a tasteless joke at a large banquet in Stamford, Connecticut. Within a year, Kiam had more than worn out his welcome in New England and placed the team up for sale.

Olson spent most of the quarter-million-dollar settlement she received from the Patriots on lawyers' fees and travel to Australia. She donated the balance to a scholarship fund for journalism students. She once described the incident as "mind rape" and refuses to discuss it except in the context of the good it inspired—that is, improved access for female reporters and better courtesy extended to them.

## THE PATRIOTS' BRIGHTEST SHINING STAR IN 1990

In the depths of the Patriots' 1–15 season in 1990, the lone bright spot was the incredible play of offensive lineman Bruce Armstrong. Not only did he make a successful transition to left tackle, but he was also named a starter in the Pro Bowl, the first of his six Pro Bowl selections. *Pro Football Weekly* also chose Armstrong to the All-AFC team. In addition, he was given the Jim Lee Hunt Award, which is presented annually to the Patriots' top interior lineman. Armstrong's heroics stood in stark contrast to the mounting losses that New England compiled throughout 1990. A decade later, in 2000, Armstrong was elected to the Patriots' All-Century team. A year after that, he was inducted into the team's Hall of Fame. His shoes are displayed at the Hall at Patriot Place.

# Rust and Ruin in 1990

Rod Rust was always known as a player's coach—or, to be more precise, a defensive player's coach—but he is also remembered in New England as possibly the worst head coach in franchise history. The dour defensive specialist seemingly put the Patriots in reverse: His team scored only 181 points to their opponents' 446.

After dropping their 1990 opening game to Miami by a score of 27–24 at Foxboro Stadium, the Patriots gave fans a glimmer of hope when they beat the Colts by a narrow 16–14 margin in Indianapolis. Any hope that the team would achieve anything of substance, however, vanished within a day of their first and only win.

The following day, three Patriots disgraced the franchise when they taunted and verbally assaulted reporter Lisa Olson. After the story broke in *The Boston Globe,* the Patriots were vilified, and soon the national media descended on Foxboro to report on what seemed like an endless saga of shame and recrimination.

The Patriots were nearly as much a disgrace on the field as off. They lost their next 14 games in a row by an average score of 29–10. They drew their only home sellout against the New York Giants on December 30 and lost 13–10. Not since the days of Ron Erhardt (2–14 in 1981) had the Patriots fallen so far. Only one Patriot, tackle Bruce Armstrong, was selected to the Pro Bowl, and the only thing fans could cheer for was the No. 1 selection in the 1991 draft.

Even Rust's name was an apt metaphor, as the coach seemed to visibly age as the season drew to a close. His press conferences were almost funereal, with the taciturn taskmaster responding to questions in somber, one-sentence answers. When *Boston Globe* reporter Frank Dell'Apa asked Rust if he objected to Eagles head coach Buddy Ryan's flamboyant style, he simply said, "The team that wins has the right approach."

Rust was fired on January 4, 1991, and Syracuse coach Dick MacPherson replaced him three days later. Within weeks, in a gesture that some viewed as symbolic of an exorcism, the team ripped up the rock-hard artificial turf at Foxboro Stadium and replaced it with natural grass.

*Rod Rust, shown here in his role as Patriots defensive coordinator in 1986, was known as both a player's coach and a superb defensive tactician. His tenure as the team's head coach became nothing less than a nightmare, however, as the Patriots finished last in the AFC East in 1990.*

*The austere Rod Rust appears on the cover of this 1990 Patriots fact book. The 1990 season, however, was not one that Patriots fans want to remember.*

# The St. Louis Patriots?

To Patriots fans, the image of owner James Busch Orthwein was that of a caricature reminiscent of *Gilligan's Island* millionaire/dilettante Thurston J. Howell. For most, he was simply the rich guy from Missouri who nearly engineered the team's relocation to St. Louis, which had lost the Cardinals to Arizona in 1988. Although the proposed move was *one* option for the former advertising executive, Orthwein should be remembered as the man who not only revitalized the Patriots on many levels but also kept the team in New England.

Orthwein came to Foxboro as the result of the NFL's insistence that Victor Kiam unload the struggling franchise in the wake of the sexual-harassment fiasco and the team's onfield implosion. Orthwein accomplished much in his short tenure as the Patriots' owner. Within his first ten months, he reestablished the team's competitive, economic, and public relations credibility. First, on January 21, 1993, the Patriots went from laughingstock to warriors at the instant Bill Parcells signed a contract to become New England's next head coach. Next, the team announced on March 31 that they would play in new electric blue and silver uniforms, which featured a new logo soon dubbed the "Flying Elvis."

Within weeks, Orthwein insisted that the team select Washington State quarterback Drew Bledsoe over the more highly touted Notre Dame quarterback Rick Mirer with the first overall pick in the 1993 NFL Draft. True to his advertising sensibilities, Orthwein had accomplished a complete makeover for his team. Soon, a flock of new season-ticket holders and sponsors paved the way for a group of prospective owners drawn to the franchise's burnished image and bright future.

As the 1993 season drew to a close, Orthwein set a year-end deadline for local prospective owners to make a bid, lest he be forced to sell the Patriots for the best offer from an interested party outside New England, which most likely would have come from St. Louis.

On January 21, 1994, Orthwein sold the Patriots to Robert Kraft for a reported sum of $168 million. "As much as I wanted a team for St. Louis," he remarked upon his departure, "this community has shown me how much it wanted to keep the Patriots here. . . . I want to tell everyone that from the day I bought the team, I tried to do the right thing. I told everyone on our staff to be guided by that single principle."

*Budweiser heir James Busch Orthwein bought the Patriots from Victor Kiam in 1992. Orthwein was the great-grandson of Anheuser-Busch founder Adolphus Busch. He was also a world-class angler.*

This 1993 vintage Patriots buggy has a die-cast body and the new Patriots logo. It is still popular among New England collectors.

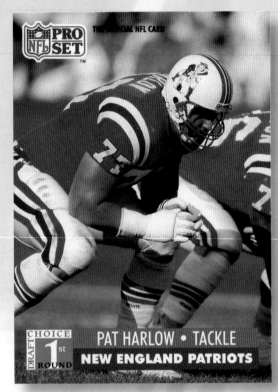

The Patriots selected offensive tackle Pat Harlow (shown on this 1991 NFL card) with the 11th overall pick of the 1991 NFL Draft. Harlow played five seasons for New England.

Patriots owner James Busch Orthwein worked with the NFL to develop the Patriots' new image, as symbolized by the new logo seen on this pin. The stylized minuteman and the team's new electric blue home uniforms were unveiled at a press conference on March 31, 1993.

The Patriots overcame the Jets, 6-3, at Giants Stadium on December 15, 1991. This program previewed this game.

This 1993 yearbook features the two men responsible for the Patriots' late 1993 resurgence—quarterback Drew Bledsoe and head coach Bill Parcells.

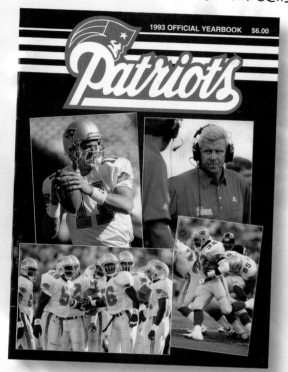

1993 OFFICIAL YEARBOOK $6.00

*Patriots*

Boston Herald reporter Lisa Olson continued to do her job, and do it well, despite the grief she endured from a few players and many fans who angrily refused to believe that she was a victim of sexual harassment in the Patriots' locker room on September 17, 1990.

Lottery player dies after hitting jackpot

By HELEN KENNEDY

A 37-year-old South Boston cafeteria cook, who last week cashed the first installment of a $3.6 million Megabucks jackpot, died of a heart attack yesterday.
Turn to Page 59

Stuart movie is too much TV, not enough reality

MONICA COLLINS

A crazy TV irony: Tune in to ABC's "thirtysomething" tonight and you'll see actor Ken Olin, overjoyed at the birth of his son.
Switch the channel to

CBS, and there's the versatile Mr. Olin, playing who murders his wife and baby son.

DIMAITI FAMILY UNHAPPY/PAGE 20

an expectant father named Charles Stuart

It's a living. It's also TV. In the end, it's only TV.
The best scenes in
Turn to Page 47

# BOSTON HERALD

35 Cents
★★★
WEATHER: PAGE 28
Partly sunny
High around 70.
TV: PAGE 46
LOTTERIES: PAGE 77
Tuesday, September 25, 1990

## Big Dig drives closer to final approval

By LAURA BROWN

New England's top federal environmental official gave the state a cautious go-ahead yesterday for the next phase of the Big Dig review process, making final approval possible by the end of this year.
In a dramatic reversal of previous comments on the Central Artery-Third Harbor Tunnel project, Environmental Protection Agency chief Julie Belaga said she now "a possibility here for a win-win situation," and referred to a "good working relation-
Turn to Page 6

## Leaders condemn Saddam at U.N.

World leaders opened a U.N. General Assembly session yesterday by condemning Iraq as a warlike state for its invasion.

SOARING OIL PRICES TOP $40 A BARREL
Business: Page 29

DOW PLUNGES 59.41 TO LOWEST IN YEAR
Business: Page 31

# NFL czar asked to sack the Pats

Sexual harass fine ripped

By ED GRAY and JACK O'LEARY

The New England Patriots closed their investigation of the sexual harassment of Boston Herald reporter Lisa Olson by five members of the team yesterday by fining one unnamed player an undisclosed amount of money.
"This is a complete whitewash and totally unacceptable" said Herald Executive Sports Editor Bob Sales. "As far as I'm concerned this is still a matter for the league to handle."
The Herald appealed to National Football League Commissioner Paul Tagliabue yesterday to take action on the sexual harassment.
"I went to (Patriots General Manager) Pat Sullivan in good

AT WORK: Herald sports reporter Lisa Olson goes about her work yesterday, interviewing Patriots wide receiver Irving Fryar in the team's Foxboro locker room. Also on hand were players Zeke Mowatt, second from right, and George Adams. Mowatt was identified by Olson as one of the players who sexually harassed her last week in the locker room.
Staff photo by Ted Ancher

INSIDE:

One of the Patriots' short-lived mascots was this lumpy figure from the 1992 season.

Patriots head coach Rod Rust is shown on the cover of the now-defunct *SportBoston* with Patriots draftees Chris Singleton and Ray Agnew.

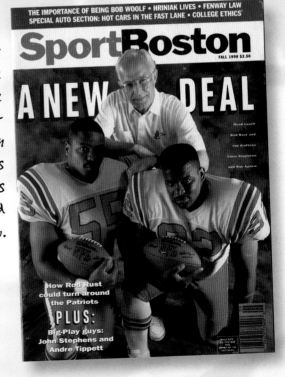

THE IMPORTANCE OF BEING BOB WOOLF • HRINIAK LIVES • FENWAY LAW
SPECIAL AUTO SECTION: HOT CARS IN THE FAST LANE • COLLEGE ETHICS

# SportBoston
FALL 1990 $2.50

# A NEW DEAL

Head coach Rod Rust and top draftees Chris Singleton and Ray Agnew

How Rod Rust could turn around the Patriots

PLUS: Big-Play guys: John Stephens and Andre Tippett

# The Big Tuna Meets the Flying Elvis

When James Busch Orthwein hired coaching legend Bill Parcells to lead the Patriots, after having also interviewed Buddy Ryan and Mike Ditka for the job, the move shocked both fans and football insiders alike. Not only were the Patriots one of the worst teams in the NFL, but they were also rumored to be headed out of New England—not exactly an ideal scenario for a coach whose doctors asked him to forsake his profession due to three heart procedures that included a quadruple bypass.

By January 1993, Parcells had given up cigarettes and peanut butter, but—after a brief stint as an NBC analyst—he couldn't resist the lure of the sideline. When he signed a lucrative five-year, $6-million contract with the Patriots, his return marked a homecoming of sorts. It had been only 13 years since Parcells had acquired the nickname "Big Tuna" while serving as the Patriots' assistant coach of linebackers. The nickname attracted national attention during Parcells's remarkable eight-year tenure as head coach of the New York Giants, during which he led the team to their first two Super Bowl titles. There was no bigger fish in either the NFL or New York City.

*The Patriots hired Super Bowl–winning coach Bill Parcells on January 21, 1993. In four seasons as head coach of the Patriots, Parcells led the team to two playoff appearances, including their second Super Bowl in 1997.*

*This Pro Magnets team magnet is from the "Heroes of the Locker Room" collection. The "Flying Elvis" logo of the New England Patriots is displayed on this 1998 piece.*

Parcells gave the Patriots instant legitimacy. His mission in New England was simple: Save a franchise that had won only 14 games during the previous four seasons. Accordingly, Parcells was granted complete control of the team.

He started by hiring eight former Giants assistant coaches and setting up a series of springtime weight and workout sessions for players. Several of the players who didn't travel east for the workouts were traded or cut. Even the sports media were subject to the rule of the Tuna and placed in a roped-off area beyond earshot of the profane taskmaster. Press conferences were held daily from 11:30 to noon; Parcells held court in a packed interview room and proved the perfect distraction for a team still trying to resolve a multitude of off-field issues.

In his first season, Parcells suffered through a horrible beginning with his new squad, seeing his Patriots lose 11 of their first 12 games. Were it not for the equally inept Phoenix Cardinals and a narrow 23–21 win at Sun Devil Stadium, the Patriots would have suffered their worst start ever. As the season wore on, many discouraged fans leapt off the bandwagon. By mid-December, the team was playing to crowds of less than 30,000 at Foxboro Stadium.

Despite the Patriots' pitiful record, Parcells rallied his team for a season-ending run of four consecutive wins, including a 38–0 blowout of the Indianapolis Colts in Foxboro. With four years remaining on his contract, Parcells was building his team for the long haul.

# Passing Fancy

After a terrible 1992 season with a 2–14 record, the Patriots looked to turn their misfortunes around and finally field a consistently competitive team. They hadn't been to the playoffs since 1986, when the Broncos knocked them out in the divisional round, and the following six seasons had brought them only a combined 31–64 record.

New England hadn't had a reliable quarterback since the Steve Grogan era, with 1992 producing one of their worst showings at the position. Four different men started behind center, and none started more than seven games. The silver lining of their 2–14 record in 1992 was the No. 1 draft pick in 1993, and the prospect of selecting a certain promising young quarterback from Washington State.

In 1992, Drew Bledsoe set single-season records at Washington State in pass completions and passing yards, earning him the title of Pac-10 Player of the Year. After his monster season, Bledsoe decided to forego his final year of college and enter the draft.

At 6'5", 200-plus pounds, and with a cannon for an arm, Bledsoe was an obvious fit for the Pats, who were in need of a strong, durable quarterback to become their new leader. The Patriots had also changed coaches again, this time hiring Bill Parcells, who hadn't coached since winning Super Bowl XXV with the Giants. Parcells was counted on to rebuild the franchise, paying special attention to developing his star quarterback.

*Following five months on the sidelines, Drew Bledsoe replaced the injured Tom Brady in the AFC championship game in Pittsburgh on January 27, 2002. Bledsoe made several key plays, including a touchdown pass to wide receiver David Patten, to help seal New England's victory.*

Bledsoe started his first game in the NFL against the Bills. The Pats would lose that game and begin the season with a 1–11 record, giving backup quarterback Scott Secules a few starts in relief of the shell-shocked rookie. But the year ended on a high note, with Bledsoe leading the team to four straight wins to finish the season. The Pats were still 5–11, and at the bottom of the AFC, but now there was reason to hope.

*Drew Bledsoe arrived in 1993 as the Patriots' most heralded savior since fellow quarterback Jim Plunkett was chosen as the NFL's first overall pick in 1971. This 1995 pennant shows how popular Bledsoe was in New England in the 1990s.*

## PATS WHO WERE PICKED NO. 1 OVERALL

**1971:** Jim Plunkett, quarterback, Stanford. Plunkett played brilliantly for New England but was never a good fit. He was traded to the 49ers for a slew of draft choices that were used to build the powerhouse teams of the 1970s.

**1982:** Ken Sims, defensive end, Texas. Some consider Sims to be the Patriots' worst-ever draft selection, never living up to his collegiate press clippings. He played only eight lackluster seasons with the Patriots.

**1984:** Irving Fryar, wide receiver, Nebraska. Fryar was one of the best athletes ever drafted by the Patriots. He became one of their best wide receivers.

**1993:** Drew Bledsoe, quarterback, Washington State. Bledsoe left the Patriots following Super Bowl XXXVI.

*Billy Sullivan and Irving Fryar*

# CHAPTER FIVE

# Salvation

## 1994–2000

*"You guys really like to hit me, don't you?"*

DOLPHIN QUARTERBACK DAN MARINO, TO
PATRIOT DEFENSIVE BACK LAWYER MILLOY

**Above:** *The Patriots' 1996 AFC championship, honored with this souvenir license plate, represented the successful start of the Robert Kraft era.* **Right:** *After receiving a pass from Drew Bledsoe, Keith Byars scampers for the end zone. The Patriots clobbered the Steelers, 28–3, in this 1996 AFC divisional playoff game.*

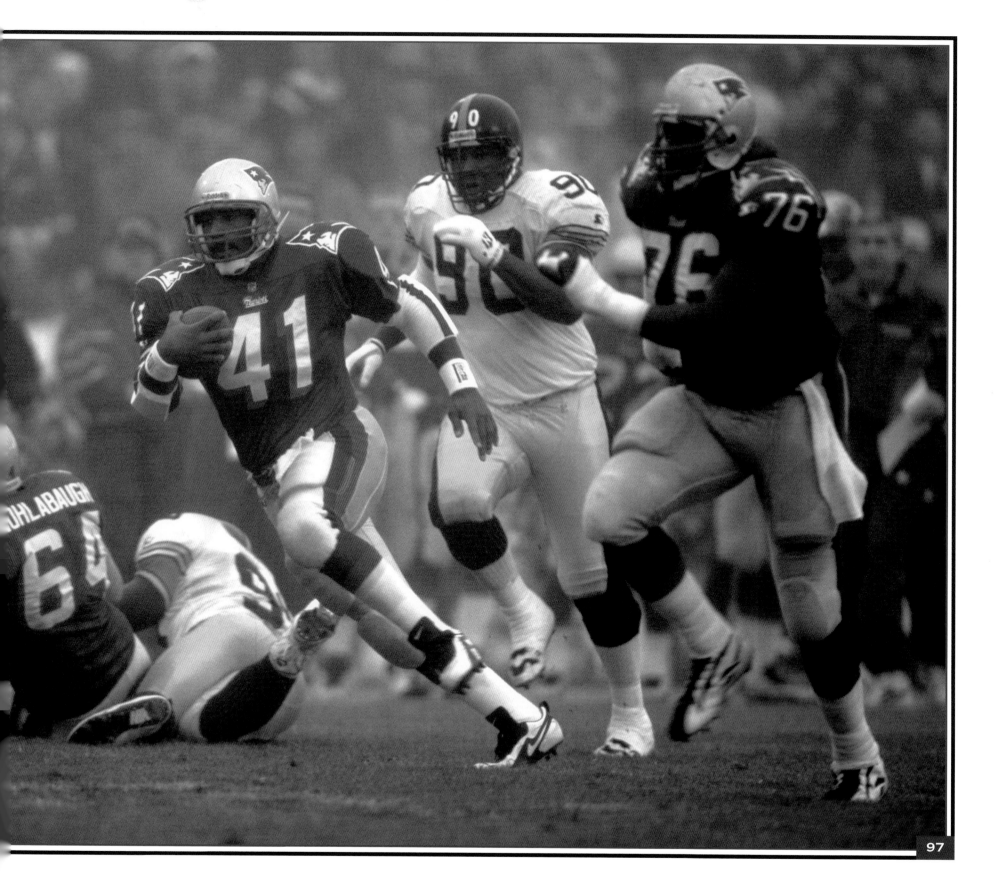

# *Kraft Saves the Day*

*T*he Patriots seemingly were gone. The newspapers had reported it, and fans felt it in their bones. On the heels of a mediocre 5–11 season, owner James Busch Orthwein issued an ultimatum stating that he would entertain serious offers from buyers willing to keep the Patriots in Foxboro—but only until December 31, 1993. Otherwise he would accept a lucrative offer he knew would come from a party in St. Louis.

Boston business executive Robert Kraft was faced with a dilemma. As owner of Foxboro Stadium and acres of adjacent property, he'd just been offered $75 million to sell the stadium and the eight years remaining on his lease to the St. Louis group. Members of his family urged him to consider the offer, which would result in a $50 million profit on his $25 million investment. Tempted as he was by the offer, he recalled how terrible he had felt when his childhood heroes, the Boston Braves, left for Milwaukee in 1953.

Having bought season tickets for many years,

*Robert Kraft went from long-suffering season-ticket holder to franchise savior in 1993. Surely he contemplated a perfect Patriots season while striding onto the field prior to Super Bowl XLII.*

Kraft was a devoted follower of the Patriots. His four sons had virtually grown up at Schaefer/Sullivan/Foxboro Stadium. Luckily for fellow fans, Kraft the Patriots fan made the ultimate decision, and not Kraft the corporate magnate.

Not only did Kraft reject the easy money, but he also met Orthwein's deadline and forced his hand as stadium leaseholder. The price was steep—$172 million, the highest price yet paid for an NFL franchise—but the Kraft family saved the Patriots.

Despite the team's woeful 5–11 record in 1993, they did win their last four games. The much-troubled franchise finally seemed headed for better times.

## FAN-DEMONIUM

It snowed on the day following the Kraft family's purchase of the Patriots. While many fans stayed inside to read their sports pages in the company of steaming mugs of coffee and hot chocolate, thousands enjoyed this day while standing in the parking lot adjacent to Foxboro Stadium. Patriots fans bought a whopping 5,958 season tickets for the 1994 season. Foxboro has been sold out since. The Patriots' season-ticket waiting list now matches the capacity of Gillette Stadium. Not bad for a team that almost moved to St. Louis.

*Foxboro Stadium in 1995*

# Back in the Saddle Again

Now that the Kraft family had bought the Patriots, would the players reward the thousands of new fans who had purchased season tickets with a winning season?

The 1994 Patriots knew they were better than the 5–11 squad that had played to half-filled grandstands at Foxboro Stadium the previous season. After all, they had finished the season with four straight victories and looked like a potential offensive powerhouse with star quarterback Drew Bledsoe in control.

The first game of the Kraft era, against Miami, was a showcase for Bledsoe and Dolphins quarterback Dan Marino. They combined for 894 passing yards and nine touchdowns in the Patriots' 39–35 loss. The offensive fireworks continued the following week, at their home opener, as New England fought back from a 35–21 fourth-quarter deficit to tie the score against Buffalo, before Steve Christie's 32-yard field goal clinched the game for the Bills. Apart from the Patriots' gallant near-miss comeback, the game was also noteworthy as it marked the first of 131 consecutive sold-out games in Foxboro through the 2008 season.

Head coach Bill Parcells regrouped his team for their next game in Cincinnati, where the Patriots rallied to beat the Bengals, 31–28, behind Bledsoe's 365 passing yards. Next, they traveled to Detroit, where they beat Barry Sanders and the Lions. They then returned home

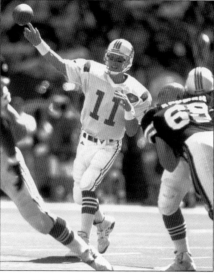

*Drew Bledsoe fires a pass in action against the Cincinnati Bengals at Riverfront Stadium in 1994. Bledsoe was the face of the franchise for half a dozen seasons, helping lead the Patriots to two Super Bowls.*

*This 1994 Patriots pennant celebrates the NFL's 75th anniversary.*

and beat the Packers, 17–16, after being down 10–0 at halftime.

The next four games, however, had fans thinking of the disastrous '93 season. The Patriots lost all four contests and soon fell to 3–6 just past the midway point of the season.

On November 13, with the Vikings holding a commanding 20–3 halftime lead at Foxboro Stadium, the Patriots seemed on their way to their fifth consecutive loss. As the third quarter kicked off, however, Parcells tossed his game plan and had Bledsoe run a no-huddle for the remainder of the game. The results were spectacular, and the Patriots rallied to tie the game on a Matt Bahr field goal with 14 seconds remaining in regulation. In overtime, the Patriots won a game for the ages, 26–20, on Bledsoe's 14-yard touchdown pass to Kevin Turner. In this game, Bledsoe set NFL records with 70 pass attempts and 45 completions.

This epic win sparked a seven-game winning streak that saw the Patriots gain their first playoff berth in eight seasons. Despite the Patriots' loss to Bill Belichick's Cleveland Browns in the wild-card game, the fans were grateful to the Krafts for saving their team for the better days they knew were to come.

*Matt Bahr kicks a field goal against the Bills in the Patriots' 41–17 victory in Buffalo in 1994. The former Giant led the Patriots in scoring in 1994 and 1995 before losing his job to Adam Vinatieri.*

# Tall Target

The football marriage of quarterback Drew Bledsoe and tight end Ben Coates was as perfect a union as any between a quarterback and receiver in modern times. At 6′5″ and 245 pounds, Coates was the ideal target for Bledsoe. Coates was also rugged enough to sustain the punishment inflicted on him in the countless short-yardage plays he completed. The lasting image of Coates for Patriots fans is that of the nimble tight end snaring Bledsoe's bullets for consecutive first downs on nearly identical pass patterns.

Coates spent nine of his ten years in the NFL with the Patriots and retired as the team's all-time leading tight end with 50 career touchdown receptions—currently good for second place, behind Stanley Morgan (67), among all Patriots receivers. Today he still ranks third in career receptions, with 490, and fourth in receiving yards, with 5,471. Upon leaving the Patriots following the 1999 season, he held the team's single-season record for receptions (96 in 1994) and the record for receptions in a single game (12 against the Colts in 1994). Coates was also an

*Ben Coates scores one of his 50 career touchdowns for the Patriots at Foxboro Stadium against Miami on November 3, 1996. In 2000, fans named Coates to the Patriots' All-Century team.*

*Tight end Ben Coates (seen here against Miami in 1993) played nine seasons for the Patriots, during which time he led the team in touchdown receptions for six consecutive seasons. In 1994, he set an NFL record for receptions (since broken) by a tight end with 96.*

iron man, playing in 113 consecutive games from 1991 to the second game of the 1998 season.

During a memorable five-year period from 1994 to 1998, Coates was unstoppable. He made the Pro Bowl in each of those seasons and helped lead the Patriots to the 1997 Super Bowl. Coates defined his position in much the same manner that other Patriot greats, such as John Hannah and Mike Haynes, had defined theirs en route to the Pro Football Hall of Fame.

In July 2008, Patriots fans elected Coates as the 13th member of the team's Hall of Fame. Prior to his induction ceremony, he recalled his special relationship with Bledsoe in a conversation with Art Martone of *The Providence Journal:* "Drew felt . . . [I was] somebody that he could depend on when the game is on the line, . . . [and] he knew where I was going to be at all times. If something broke down or didn't go the way it was supposed to go he knew exactly where I was going to be, so it worked out for him and also for me."

# Curtis Martin's Golden Season

**H**ad it not been for the severely sprained ankle he suffered in the University of Pittsburgh's second game in 1994, running back Curtis Martin likely would have been a first-round pick in the 1995 NFL Draft. When the Patriots selected him in the third round with the 74th overall pick, it was the team's biggest draft-day steal since choosing wide receiver Troy Brown in the eighth round of the 1993 draft.

Martin joined a team that had just allowed veteran running backs Marion Butts, Leroy Thompson, and Kevin Turner to depart as free agents. Head coach Bill Parcells expected Martin to bolster his running attack, and at the conclusion of training camp remarked to *The New York Times,* "He seems to have taken to pro football fairly well, and I like his athletic ability. But I think we're a little presumptuous about how he's going to do here."

These would become famous last words, for Martin was about to embark on one of the greatest rookie seasons in league history.

When observed within the realm of raw statistics, Martin's rookie season shines as one of the best in Patriots history. His NFL debut versus the Cleveland Browns at Foxboro set the tone for his breakthrough season, with Martin gaining 102 yards on 19 carries and scoring a touchdown in the Patriots' 17–14 victory.

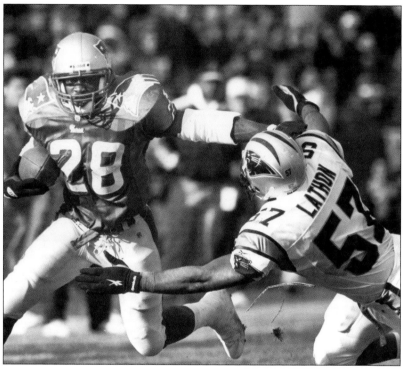

*With 1,487 yards in the 1995 season, running back Curtis Martin set what was then a Patriots single-season rushing record. He also captured NFL Offensive Rookie of the Year honors that year. Here he runs around Carolina's Lamar Lathon on October 29, 1995.*

Martin sputtered only briefly in the first half of the season when he gained just eight yards on six attempts versus the Broncos on October 8. He wouldn't reach the 100-yard mark again until his 127-yard effort against Buffalo on October 23.

Over the final ten games of the season, Martin rushed for an average of 120 yards per game. This earned the halfback NFL Offensive Rookie of the Year honors, as well as a Pro Bowl berth. In the process, Martin set what was then a Patriots single-season record of 1,487 yards, gained on 368 rushing attempts. His 14 rushing touchdowns remain a team record (which he tied in 1996).

In his two final seasons with the Patriots, 1996 and 1997, Martin led the team in rushing and net yards gained from scrimmage. As of 2008, he remained as the fourth-leading rusher in team history, and his 32 touchdowns tied him for fifth on the Patriots' all-time list. Following the 1997 season, he signed with the New York Jets as a restricted free agent for a staggering $36 million over six years.

He retired after the 2006 season, having established Hall of Fame credentials as the fourth-leading rusher in NFL history (with 14,101 yards), behind Emmitt Smith, Walter Payton, and Barry Sanders.

# Simply Super in '96

*T*he Patriots' path to their second Super Bowl was bumpy to say the least. When Robert Kraft overruled head coach Bill Parcells by selecting Ohio State wide receiver Terry Glenn with the seventh overall pick of the 1996 NFL Draft, it both ensured Parcells's imminent departure and yet motivated the two-time Super Bowl–winning coach to work even harder to create a lasting legacy in Foxboro.

This scenario was similar to that surrounding the departure of head coach Chuck Fairbanks, who had plotted his exit after the team retracted the contract offers he had made to All-Pro linemen John Hannah and Leon Gray prior to the 1977 season. The only difference was that Fairbanks jumped ship prior to losing the Patriots' first-ever home playoff game, while Parcells waited until the week of the Super Bowl for his agent to spill the beans.

The Patriots opened the 1996 season with consecutive road losses to Miami and Buffalo. Fans wondered whether the Patriots would improve on their 6–10 record from the previous season. Following a lopsided 31–0 win in their home opener against Arizona, they won five of their next six games, including a dramatic 28–25 win against Jacksonville at home. Fans were much encouraged.

Also included in this streak were gut-check wins against the Bills and the Jets. In the first game, Buffalo came back from a 13–0 halftime deficit in Foxboro to grab an 18–15 lead, thanks to a Thurman Thomas touchdown and a Darick Holmes two-point conversion. The Patriots regained the lead on Curtis Martin's ten-yard touchdown run, only to sag slightly when Adam Vinatieri's extra point sailed wide.

*After winning the 1996 AFC East title, the Patriots beat the Steelers and Jaguars to become AFC champions, as displayed on this vintage button.*

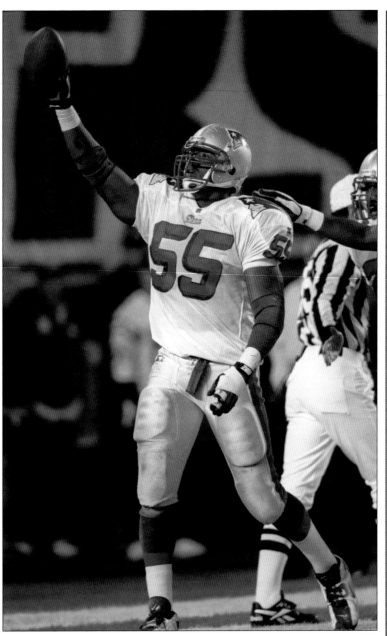

*Linebacker Willie McGinest celebrates his touchdown, scored on a fumble recovery during the Patriots' 45–7 victory against the San Diego Chargers at Jack Murphy Stadium on December 1, 1996.*

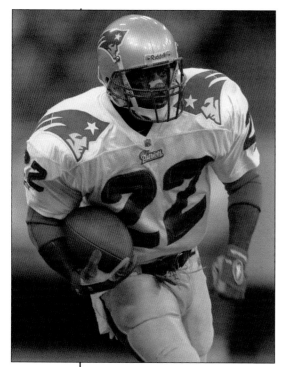

*Running back Dave Meggett was a favorite of Patriots head coach Bill Parcells, having followed his mentor from the New York Giants. In three seasons with New England, the versatile back led the team in both punt and kickoff returns.*

New England increased its lead to 28–18 when Willie McGinest intercepted a Jim Kelly pass and ran 46 yards for a touchdown. With 33 seconds to go, Kelly heaved a Hail Mary pass that deflected off several Patriot defenders into the hands of receiver Andre Reed for a highlight-reel touchdown. Following Buffalo's failed onside kick attempt, New England won, 28–25, and more than a few Patriots fans believed that maybe their team could make it back to the playoffs.

This belief was confirmed at Giants Stadium on November 10, when New England erased a double-digit deficit against the Jets with several daring plays. The most crucial was a fourth-down pass from Drew Bledsoe to Ben Coates for a first down late in the fourth quarter. Bledsoe soon followed with a two-yard touchdown pass to Keith Byars to give New England a 31–27 lead. On the next possession, New York marched as far as the Patriots' 11-yard line before Lawyer Milloy picked off a Frank Reich pass to seal the Patriots' seventh victory.

Following a devastating 34–8 home loss to Denver, their ninth straight to the Broncos, the Patriots cruised to their first division title in ten seasons by winning four of their last five games, including an unforgettable regular-season finale against the Giants in which they scored 23 unanswered points, capped by Dave Meggett's 60-yard punt-return touchdown for a 23–22 victory.

The 1996 Patriots benefited from some of the greatest coaching in franchise history. Backed by the Pro Bowl performances of Bledsoe, offensive tackle Bruce Armstrong, tight end Ben Coates, running back Curtis Martin, defensive end Willie McGinest, and kick-return specialist Dave Meggett, Parcells tutored a host of first- and second-year players—such as Ty Law, Lawyer Milloy, Ted Johnson, and Tedy Bruschi—in the art of winning.

Although the Patriots succumbed to the Green Bay Packers in Super Bowl XXXI, 35–21, the 1996 team established the foundation for the dynasty that followed. The team also established the Krafts as owners of the first rank, while at the same time informing them of the potential drawbacks inherent in adopting too great a hands-on approach. In time, the lessons learned both on and off the field by the 1996 team allowed the Krafts to write a history altogether different from their predecessors' tortured tales.

*Wide receiver Terry Glenn was team owner Robert Kraft's choice as the Patriots' first-round selection in the 1996 NFL Draft. Glenn made an immediate impact, setting an NFL rookie record with his 90 receptions. Here he faces the Colts in 1996.*

License plates that proclaimed the Patriots as 1996 AFC champions could be seen throughout New England.

The 1996 Patriots season-ticket holders proudly proclaimed their exclusive status with this lapel pin.

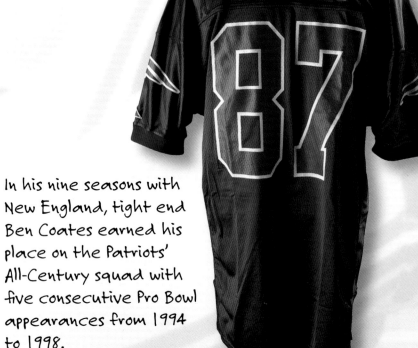

In his nine seasons with New England, tight end Ben Coates earned his place on the Patriots' All-Century squad with five consecutive Pro Bowl appearances from 1994 to 1998.

The wide range of Patriots collectibles includes this die-cast bank, which is a replica of a 1951 GMC panel truck.

By 1996, Patriots fans could once again be proud of their team. Some chose to show that pride by hanging Patriots ornaments, such as this Hallmark piece.

Headlining a December 9, 1996, issue of the *Boston Herald*, the Patriots punched their playoff ticket in game 14, a 34-10 victory against the Jets at Foxboro Stadium.

GAME 14: THE JETS

# Pats' clinch a cinch

Dump Jets to earn playoff bid

By KEVIN MANNIX

PLAYOFF SMILE: Troy Brown shows a happy face to the fans as he walks to the locker room after the Patriots clinched a playoff berth with a 34-10 win over the New York Jets yesterday.

Quarterback Drew Bledsoe established himself as a Pro Bowl performer and achieved immortality as a Starting Lineup figure in his second season as a Patriot.

The 1994 Patriots sold carloads of pennants, as well as other souvenirs, after they reached the playoffs for the first time in nine seasons.

# Going Long

Although Drew Bledsoe finished his days with the Patriots as a Super Bowl champ, he didn't ride off into the sunset. Rather, he was a victim of evolution, having been replaced by a stronger, fitter Tom Brady. More than a few Pats fans have joked about Bledsoe's immobility in the pocket, and spending three seasons with Buffalo following his departure from the Patriots certainly didn't help cement his legacy in New England. But Bledsoe is still the Patriots' all-time leader in passing yards, and he was the face of the franchise throughout most of the 1990s. Bledsoe was one of the last quarterbacks in the league who was a pure thrower. He never made plays with his feet, nor could he scramble away from defenders, but Bledsoe could simply throw a football harder and more accurately than most who ever played the position.

In Bledsoe's second season in 1994, at age 22, head coach Bill Parcells decided to make up for the team's lack of a running game with Bledsoe's arm, setting the record for most passing attempts in one season. Parcells seemingly took a big risk with his game plan, because most young quarterbacks would not be able to handle the heavy workload, mentally or physically. But Bledsoe's athletic ability and talents at quarterback made him the exception.

Bledsoe's Pro Bowl–worthy sophomore campaign, however, was not without its problems. He piled up 4,555 yards and 25 touchdowns, but he also finished with 27 interceptions and a not-so-sterling 73.6 quarterback rating. But the bottom line from that playoff season was that Bledsoe could handle the pressures of being quarterback, that he could win football games, and that he showed flashes of brilliance.

One of those performances came in week 11 of the '94 season, with the Pats, at 3–6, playing Minnesota at home. The home team gave up 20 quick points to the Vikings, and Parcells decided to go with a no-huddle offense in the middle of the game to jump-start the team. The Pats tacked on a field goal before halftime, but they were still down 20–3. Parcells let Bledsoe go wild. Bledsoe then set NFL records for completions and pass attempts in one game,

with 45 and 70, respectively. He finished with 426 yards and three TDs, including the game-winner in overtime to fullback Kevin Turner, capping off the 26–20 comeback. That win would turn the season around for the Pats—the team went on to win the rest of their regular-season games and reach the playoffs—and the performance would lift expectations for Bledsoe through the roof.

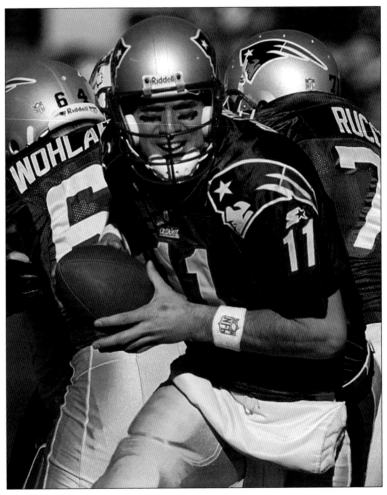

*Drew Bledsoe drops back to pass in the Patriots' 17–3 AFC wild-card victory against the Miami Dolphins at Foxboro Stadium on December 28, 1997.*

# Team of Innovation

The Patriots are as much a creation of Harvard Business School as they are of such noted football factories as Notre Dame, Alabama, USC, Michigan, Oklahoma, and Ohio State (to name but a few). For it was at Harvard Business School that Robert Kraft and son Jonathan learned the intricacies of a playbook every bit as complex and challenging as anything devised by coaches Bill Parcells or Bill Belichick.

The Krafts have not only recast the former NFL laughingstock as formidable champions but have also created a revolutionary business plan. This plan ensures that the Patriots maximize unrestricted income while operating an entertainment entity as compelling to fans in the cheap seats as to shrimp-eating, suite-bound corporate moguls.

Shortly after they purchased the team, the Krafts decided to upgrade their radio broadcasts markedly by moving them from the traditional AM band to the crystal-clear sound of FM. By selecting Boston's traditional rock 'n' roll flagship station, WBCN, they guaranteed that the Patriots would have newfound appeal among young listeners, as well as entice older listeners attracted by their broadcast's improved production values. They also retained veteran play-by-play announcer Gil Santos and Patriot legend Gino Cappelletti, in recognition of both their excellence and the team's appreciation of the best aspects of Patriots heritage.

In February 1995, the Patriots selected Boston's local ABC affiliate, WCVB, to televise their preseason games and a magazine-style program

*Gillette Stadium opened in 2002 as home to both the Patriots and the New England Revolution of Major League Soccer. The stadium also serves as the hub of Patriot Place, a major retail and entertainment development.*

*Workers place the letters on the facade of Gillette Stadium in August 2002. Originally dubbed CMGI Field, the stadium was renamed after the company's setback in the dot-com bust.*

entitled *Patriots All-Access.* Later that same year, the team also launched *Patriots Football Weekly,* the third team newspaper in the NFL, following similar publications issued by the Cowboys and Giants. Within two years, the Patriots were mailing it to subscribers in every state, as well as to countless fans around the world.

In yet another move to inform fans, the Patriots introduced the world's first-ever direct-to-digital nightly video Webcast on August 25, 1997. Included in this groundbreaking program were player interviews, press conferences, and game previews/reviews.

All of these innovations served as merely the prelude to a multistage process that started with the 68,000-seat Gillette Stadium opening in Foxboro in 2002. Within half a dozen years, the stadium was followed by the construction of a mammoth retail/entertainment complex known as "Patriot Place," which opened in 2008. Among the more noteworthy attractions of Patriot Place are a team museum and an expansive Bass Pro Shops store.

# Home Cooking

The Patriots finished the 1996 regular season with an 11–5 record, good enough to grant them a bye through the first round of the playoffs and initial home-field advantage, the first time they would host a playoff game since 1978. They would face the Pittsburgh Steelers, who had won the AFC Central Division and defeated Indianapolis convincingly in the wild-card round, 42–14.

On the Sunday morning of the game, a thick fog rolled into Foxboro Stadium. These conditions favored the Steelers and their powerful ground attack, led by Jerome Bettis. Despite two bad ankles, Bettis had managed a 102-yard, two-touchdown performance against the Colts a week earlier and could be counted on to be the Steelers' workhorse, especially in short-yardage situations. On the other side of the ball, the Pittsburgh defense had shut down almost every running back they faced.

Once the game started, however, the Pats went right after the Steelers on offense *and* defense. After Pittsburgh's offense stalled on their first drive, the Pats used their good field position and a 53-yard connection between Drew Bledsoe and Terry Glenn to set up a Curtis Martin TD run, all within the first minute of the game. The Pats' defense shut down Pittsburgh early on, forcing the Steelers to punt away their first nine possessions. While the Steelers' offensive crew made themselves at home on the bench, Bledsoe continued to lead the charge. He had another big pass play, this time 34 yards to Keith Byars for a score. Martin and the Pats' blockers caught the Steelers in a blitz, and the running back was able to rush by them for a huge 78-yard run right to the end zone. At halftime the score was 21–0.

Parcells eased up on the play calls in the second half, not wanting to press his team's luck. Pittsburgh managed a field goal in the third quarter but was otherwise helpless on offense. Quarterback Mike Tomczak threw two interceptions, while his backup, Kordell Stewart, went 0 for 10 on passing attempts. Bettis irritated a lingering groin injury and was taken out, adding injury to insult.

*Cornerback Ty Law (No. 24) leaps to break up a pass intended for Steeler wide receiver Yancey Thigpen.*

The Patriots stopped throwing the long ball in the second half, and Martin continued to run well, piling up 166 yards and adding another touchdown run to close out the game. What was supposed to be a close, hard-fought game turned into a 28–3 romp, which certainly made the Patriots look capable of becoming the next AFC champions.

# AFC Glory

After unseating the defending AFC champions, the Pittsburgh Steelers, in the 1996 playoffs, the Patriots were feeling confident going into another game at home, this time against the surprising Jacksonville Jaguars. The two teams had met before in week four at New England, with the Patriots earning a slim 28–25 overtime victory.

The Jaguars had been in existence for only two seasons, having entered the NFL with the Carolina Panthers in 1995. Traditionally, expansion franchises had taken at least five years to develop into playoff contenders. But the NFL, now wanting competitive parity among all their clubs, took strides to make certain the new teams would come out of the gate hot. In the 1995 NFL Draft, Jacksonville and Carolina traded off first and second picks in all rounds. Along with supplemental picks in the later rounds, they wound up with 14 selections each, twice what

*Head coach Bill Parcells receives the traditional victory bath from his Patriots players after beating the Jaguars, 20–6, to capture the 1996 AFC championship.*

the other teams received in the seven-round draft.

With their influx of young talent, a no-nonsense coach in Tom Coughlin, and a smart trade to land Brett Favre's backup, Mark Brunell, the Jaguars had what it took to be a winning team right off the bat. The Jaguars' first two playoff wins, on the road at Buffalo and Denver,

with identical 30–27 scores, more than validated their place in the league. In Foxboro, the Jags were lucky enough not to see any fog, as the Steelers had, or New England's dreaded snow, but the whole stadium faced one problem early on. Halfway through the second quarter, the lights at Foxboro Stadium went out, leaving everyone in the dark. The power was restored after about ten minutes, and the incident was the only New England failure of the day.

The Patriots got things going early with a goal-line touchdown run from running back Curtis Martin. They also added two Adam Vinatieri field goals before the half to take the lead, 13–3. Mike Hollis kicked another field goal for Jacksonville in the third quarter, pulling the Jaguars to within a touchdown. But Patriot Otis Smith was able to grab a Jaguar fumble and race 47 yards to the end zone late in the fourth quarter to seal the win.

The Pats didn't blow the Jags away, but the offense played a smart game, and the defense shut down Brunell and the Jaguar offense. The Patriots played like the team they had become—the AFC champions. They had now set themselves up for a trip to New Orleans, the site of their first Super Bowl appearance, for a chance to finally bring the Super Bowl trophy to New England.

*On January 12, 1997, the Patriots clinched the AFC championship at Foxboro Stadium with a 20–6 victory against Jacksonville. The game was previewed in this Game Day program.*

*Curtis Martin scores a first-quarter touchdown against Jacksonville in the AFC championship game.*

# *Another Super Loss*

*T*he Patriots were riding high after their two big playoff wins in January 1997, and they were feeling all the love that the zealous sports fans around New England usually reserved for the Red Sox, Bruins, and Celtics. The Pats had enjoyed a winning season here and there during their checkered history, but now they had become a successful franchise.

The Pats had the pieces of a great team, and they were about to face their greatest challenge of the 1996 season—the Green Bay Packers, who had finished the regular season with an NFC-best 13–3 record. The Packers had taken care of the formidable 49ers and Panthers at their home, Lambeau Field, with relative ease to reach the big game.

That season, the Packers were one of the few teams in NFL history to lead the entire league in both points scored and points allowed. Brett Favre guided the team at quarterback, throwing an incredible 39 touchdowns during the regular season. The Packers' league-best defense featured Pro Bowlers Reggie White at defensive end and LeRoy Butler at safety. Return man Desmond

*Safety Larry Whigham expresses the deflated spirit of the Patriots bench as he covers his eyes in the final minutes of New England's 35–21 Super Bowl loss to the Green Bay Packers on January 26, 1997.*

*Wide receiver Terry Glenn makes one of his four receptions against the Packers in Super Bowl XXXI as defensive back Eugene Robinson makes the tackle.*

Howard loomed as a constant threat to strike for a big gain on a punt or kick return. The Packers were certainly the best team in the league heading to the Super Bowl, and they were given a 14-point advantage by oddsmakers going into the game. Nevertheless, the Patriots and their fans went to New Orleans with a quiet confidence.

Green Bay took off right out of the gate, scoring on a long 54-yard pass from Favre to Andre Rison on the second offensive play of the game. Kicker Chris Jacke added a 37-yard field goal shortly after that to give Green Bay a ten-point lead. The Pats responded with a couple of long touchdown drives, which were capped with Bledsoe's scoring passes to Keith Byars and then to Ben Coates. At the end of the first quarter, New England led, 14–10. The Patriots were proving what their fans were

On their way to Super Bowl XXXI, the Patriots matched the 11-5 regular-season record of the 1985 AFC champion Patriots. This pennant hung in homes in New England after the 1996 season.

The late NFL commissioner Pete Rozelle is honored with this memorial tribute on the cover of the program for Super Bowl XXXI.

On January 26, 1997, New England fans celebrate their team in New Orleans before entering the Superdome for Super Bowl XXXI.

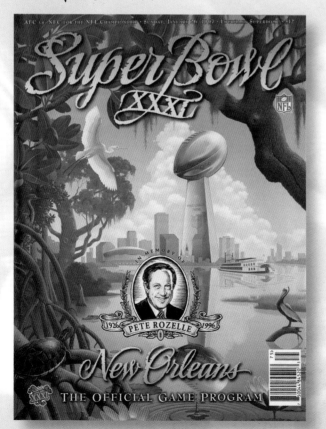

Young Patriots fans played with the action figures of Drew Bledsoe, Curtis Martin, Dave Meggett, Keith Byars, and Ben Coates—if their parents didn't pre-serve the toys as collectibles first.

# Hail and Farewell

When Robert Kraft paid $172 million for the Patriots, he purchased the doormat of the NFL, as well as the services of its most charismatic and dynamic coach, Bill Parcells. It should have been a marriage made in heaven, but instead it was a shotgun union of well-intentioned but incompatible alpha males.

Their relationship quickly became a favorite topic for Boston's sports media, and writers openly speculated how long the two could stay together. Parcells, especially, had to be in control. Not only did the former Giants legend possess two Super Bowl rings, but he was also proud owner of the stare that launched a thousand press conferences. Parcells could stop most men dead at 20 paces with that stare.

A tough kid from Jersey, Parcells had been coached in high school by a taskmaster named Mickey Cochrane, whom a fledgling coach named Vince Lombardi had tutored. If coaching bloodlines mean anything, Parcells's coaching style came from arguably the greatest coach of all. And for three decades, Parcells was known as both a master motivator and psychologist.

Players lived in fear of his rebukes and craved his slightest compliment. His commitment to his craft was well documented, having contributed to at least one heart attack and countless recommendations from doctors to retire from the sidelines. Meanwhile, his presence in Foxboro made the Patriots credible, and in four seasons he brought them to the top of the AFC.

On the eve of the 1996 draft, Parcells decided to leave the Patriots after learning the team would draft wide receiver Terry Glenn against his wishes. He later told *Boston Globe* columnist and confidant Will McDonough, "I'm not leaving here 6–10. I'm going to come back here and prove I'm better than that. I did a lousy job [in 1995]. I know that. But next year we've got a chance to be pretty good."

Following Super Bowl XXXI, he bade farewell to the Patriots and remarked, "If they want you to cook the dinner, they ought to let you buy the groceries."

*Every NFL head coach finds losing deeply painful. For Bill Parcells, losing is especially agonizing, and the Patriots' 1995 season was full of agonizing moments.*

# Hanging Loose with Pete Carroll

*I*n the wake of the successful but authoritarian reign of Bill Parcells, the Patriots replaced Jack Nicholson with Mister Rogers in the person of former Jets head coach and 49ers defensive coordinator Pete Carroll. Carroll came to Foxboro with a mediocre record but with glowing recommendations from the likes of Bill Walsh and George Seifert. Most important, the enthusiastic and likable Marin County native was the anti-Parcells, the ultimate player's coach.

Despite the Patriots' Super Bowl season, the 1996 team began to disintegrate even before losing to the Packers. Not only had Parcells made his exit strategy known prior to the game, but his destination was the head coaching job of the hated New York Jets. Long before "The Big Tuna" crossed the Jersey state line, the chorus of criticism was echoing from the Foxboro Stadium locker room.

*Following the authoritarian rule of Bill Parcells, Patriots players welcomed Pete Carroll as head coach in 1997, viewing Carroll as a player's coach.*

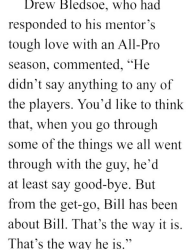

*Pete Carroll brought a laid-back persona to his duties as Patriots head coach. He led the Patriots to the AFC East division title in 1997 and a wild-card appearance in 1998.*

Drew Bledsoe, who had responded to his mentor's tough love with an All-Pro season, commented, "He didn't say anything to any of the players. You'd like to think that, when you go through some of the things we all went through with the guy, he'd at least say good-bye. But from the get-go, Bill has been about Bill. That's the way it is. That's the way he is."

It didn't take long for the kinder, gentler Carroll to experience a similar backlash. Simply put, Carroll was too nice and trusting for his own good. Sportswriter Dan Pires likened him to a substitute teacher who had inherited an unruly classroom in a tough neighborhood. Carroll forfeited a measure of his authority by joining the team's intramural basketball league, and he tried too hard to gain his team's affection before they had begun to respect him. In retrospect, however, he never had a chance.

It didn't help that Parcells loomed large as the Jets' head coach. While Carroll took the AFC champions to disappointing playoff appearances in both 1997 and 1998, and a mediocre 8–8 record in 1999, Parcells's Jets enjoyed their best performances since the days of "Broadway" Joe Namath.

In three seasons as head coach, Carroll won more games than either Parcells or Belichick did in their first three years in Foxboro. It didn't matter. Within a day after the 1999 Patriots won their season finale against the Ravens, New England fired Carroll. He bade farewell to the NFL, explaining, "I'm proud of being 27–21 and making the playoffs the first two years I was here. I'll forever be disappointed we didn't win more."

# *Playoff Trauma*

*T*hey were the "almost" team. They were also one of the most exciting teams in Patriots history, and certainly the most perplexing. With the bitter memory of their Super Bowl loss to Green Bay fresh in their minds, the 1997 Pats sought to make amends.

Led by new coach Pete Carroll, the Patriots won their first four games, including a dramatic 27–24 overtime victory in Foxboro against the hated Jets, coached by former mentor Bill Parcells. The remainder of their season was nearly as exciting, a roller-coaster ride that featured a three-game losing streak at midseason and a Garrison finish of four wins in their last five games to win the AFC East.

While the Patriots prepared to host the Dolphins in the opening round of the playoffs, fans wondered which Patriot team would appear in the postseason. With the injured Curtis Martin watching in street clothes from the sidelines, the Patriots did nothing less

than pull off, in the words of sports-writer Nick Cafardo, "a legal mass-mugging of Marino and the Dolphins" in a 17–3 wild-card victory. Not only did the Patriots sack Dan Marino four times, but they also pressured him nine times, knocked down six passes, deflected four others, and intercepted him twice. As the game drew to a close, Marino looked up at Patriot defensive back Lawyer Milloy and remarked, "You guys really like to hit me, don't you?"

The following week, at Three Rivers Stadium, the Patriot defense once again played heroically, this time against the Steelers in a rematch of the previous season's divisional championship. The Patriot offense, however, was further depleted when Martin was joined on the sidelines by receivers Terry Glenn and Ben Coates.

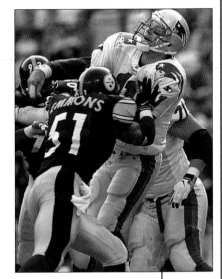

*Steeler Carlos Emmons slams into Drew Bledsoe just as he releases the football. Despite the Pats' hopes of winning another AFC title, Pittsburgh edged New England 7–6 in the 1997 division playoffs on January 3, 1998.*

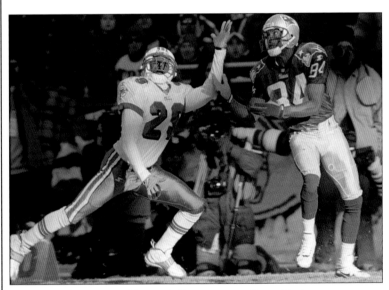

*Patriots wide receiver Shawn Jefferson eyes a Drew Bledsoe pass—as Dolphins defensive back Sam Madison prepares to break it up—in the fourth quarter of the Patriots' 17–3 AFC wild-card victory on December 28, 1997.*

With 3:24 remaining, Bledsoe took over at his own 1-yard line with the game on the line. He managed to drive to the 34-yard line, needing only to get his team in range for an Adam Vinatieri field goal. Yet, as Bledsoe rolled out on first down, he fumbled the football after being hit from behind while scanning the field for an open receiver. With two minutes remaining, the Patriots' Super Bowl hopes died once again.

Correspondent Bob Ryan described the team perfectly when he wrote, "They started the season as the '61 Yankees. They finished as the '66 Dodgers." If only their offense had avoided just one of their many late-season injuries and had matched the intensity displayed by their defense. If only . . .

# Miracle of Miracles

The 1998 football season was the best of times and worst of times for Patriots halfback Robert Edwards. Selected with the 18th overall pick of the 1998 NFL Draft, the University of Georgia star more than lived up to expectations when he led the team in rushing.

Named to the Pro Bowl All-Rookie team, Edwards traveled to Hawaii, where he would play in the rookie four-on-four flag football game at Waikiki Beach.

The most innocuous activities too often lead to the worst tragedies. Such was the case for Edwards, who, after leaping to deflect a pass, fell awkwardly to the sand, severely twisting his knee. Although he felt no immediate pain as he lay on the sand, he knew he would need a stretcher and possibly an ambulance. He later told *Sports Illustrated* that the pain felt like "dislocating your finger times 50" when it first hit him on the ride to Honolulu's Straub Clinic and Hospital.

Edwards's injuries were later described by University of Georgia sports medicine director Ronald Courson as "the worst knee injury I have ever seen." The running back tore three of his left knee's four major ligaments—his ACL, MCL, and PCL—and sustained a smaller tear to the fourth. More important, he had also nearly severed the main artery supplying blood to his lower leg.

Edwards wept as doctors informed him he might lose the leg to amputation if the sutures connecting the artery ruptured. He was also informed that his football career was over.

*In the midst of his incredible rookie season, Robert Edwards scored two touchdowns against Kansas City in the Patriots' victory at Foxboro Stadium on October 11, 1998.*

If the fact that Edwards kept his leg was a medical miracle, then his return to football after two torturous years of rehab was a miracle of miracles. His comeback attempt became the inspirational highlight of the 2001 training camp that forged the Patriots' first Super Bowl championship. Despite being cut after a full month in camp, Edwards persisted in his pursuit of his NFL dream and made the roster of the Miami Dolphins in 2002.

In his first game for the Dolphins, he scored two touchdowns, one rushing and one receiving, as teammates and fans brushed aside tears. Limited to part-time duty, Edwards lasted the entire season in Miami before being given his release.

Edwards then turned to the Canadian Football League (CFL), where he starred for the Montreal Alouettes, rushing for more than 1,000 yards and being named a CFL All-Star in 2005 and 2006. "Bigger fields, smaller crowds, wide receivers in motion like it's a fire drill or something," Edwards mused on his experiences in Canada. "But you know what? It's football. And, if you love playing, hey, why not?"

*Running back Robert Edwards enjoyed an outstanding rookie season in 1998, rushing for 1,115 yards and nine touchdowns. Here he stiff-arms Steeler defenders on December 6, 1998.*

# House Hunting with the Krafts

*T*he one truism that has characterized Boston for most of its nearly 400-year history is that all politics are local. The second truism holds that you at least double both your budget and schedule for any project, provided you start the project in the first place.

Brookline High graduate Robert Kraft was well aware of the hurdles he and his family would face when they sought to replace their outmoded stadium in Foxboro with an edifice worthy of the commitment both his family and fans had made to the Patriots. Shortly after the Krafts purchased the Patriots in 1994, NFL commissioner Paul Tagliabue told them that "Foxboro is an unacceptable venue for the long-term future of the Patriots franchise."

In other NFL markets, owners like Art Modell of the Baltimore Ravens were rewarded with newly built stadiums, complete with parking, training facilities, and seemingly endless streams of concession and luxury suite revenue. While the Krafts knew that Massachusetts would never build them such a home, they held hope that they would at least be welcomed with open arms in the best sports city in the world.

Timing is everything, and as the Patriots marched toward a January 26, 1997, Super Bowl date with the Packers, inquiries were made regarding a possible move back to the team's original home of Boston. Several sites seemed viable, including one in Somerville, roughly six miles from downtown Boston. Another, more promising site was alongside the Gillette plant and South Station Postal Annex in South Boston. Another waterfront location in South Boston was proposed as the site of a joint Red Sox/Patriots home.

The worst features of Boston politics materialized, however, as the Krafts were cast as community-wrecking carpetbaggers

*Originally christened CMGI Field, the Patriots' new home opened as a soccer venue in the spring of 2002, several months prior to both the Patriots' home opener and the renaming of the venue as Gillette Stadium in August.*

*On December 9, 1998, Patriots owners Robert* (right) *and Jonathan Kraft field questions from the Connecticut legislature as they discuss their proposed plans for the Patriots' move to Hartford.*

and worse. Massachusetts House Speaker Tom Finneran even alluded to Robert Kraft in a radio interview as "a fat-assed millionaire" seeking to take advantage of tax dollars. At the time, Kraft was willing to sink hundreds of millions of his own dollars into a run-down industrial neighborhood, while only seeking infrastructure improvements on the roads and real estate adjacent to his proposed venue. Only Massachusetts governor William Weld voiced his unequivocal support. One can only imagine the reaction if the Patriots had been in last place.

At the same time that Kraft was being vilified in Boston, officials in both Providence, Rhode Island, and Hartford, Connecticut, contacted him, seeking to land the Patriots for their respective cities. While officials in Boston stalled on their decision, Kraft soon entered into an agreement with Connecticut governor John Rowland to relocate the Patriots to a site in Hartford known as Adrien's Landing for the start of the 2001 season. The deal, valued at a cool billion, was staggering. It guaranteed both the construction of a stadium and stadium-related income. It was easily the best offer ever made to attract an NFL franchise.

Upon closer scrutiny, however, the deal contained major flaws, including the fact that the stadium was slated for construction on a hazardous waste site. That factor alone would have sidetracked

the deal for years, or at least until John Rowland left office (he was soon indicted on corruption charges, found guilty, and served ten months in a federal prison from 2005 to 2006).

Five months after the press conference announcing the Patriots' move, the Krafts exercised an exit clause and backed away from the agreement on the basis that the stadium couldn't be finished in time for the 2002 season. In time, the Commonwealth of Massachusetts responded to pressure from the NFL, area business leaders, and fans, committing to a loan of $57 million for infrastructure costs connected to the privately financed $300-million stadium. Meanwhile, in Hartford, Governor Rowland accused the Krafts of using him to leverage a better deal in Massachusetts.

The NFL ultimately paid a $2.4-million settlement to the state of Connecticut, and Foxboro's Gillette Stadium site continues to grow as the venue for a vast retail and entertainment complex.

*The Patriots' 2002 home opener, held on September 9 before a capacity crowd of 68,436, was a gala event that celebrated both the formal opening of Gillette Stadium and the unveiling of the franchise's first world championship banner.*

By the late '90s, Patriots posters such as this one signaled the team's stature as one of America's favorite NFL teams.

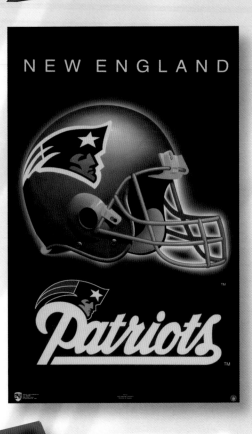

The Patriots defeated the 49ers, 20–0, at the 2000 Hall of Fame exhibition game in Canton, Ohio. Many fans at the game wore this T-shirt.

This 1999 media guide provided high hopes for the Patriots, but they ran out of gas during the season, losing six of their last eight games to finish with a mediocre 8–8 record.

Running back Robert Edwards shows his astounding leaping ability during the Pinnacle NFL Rookie Shoot in Orlando, Florida, on May 20, 1998.

The shoes of quarterback Drew Bledsoe were among the toughest in Patriots history to fill. The former top overall pick in the 1993 NFL Draft was voted by fans to the Patriots' All-Century team in 2000.

This 1998 media guide features 1997 Patriots Pro Bowlers Bruce Armstrong, Drew Bledsoe, Ben Coates, Chris Slade, and Larry Whigham on its cover.

NEW ENGLAND **PATRIOTS**

MEDIA GUIDE

**20 00**

A NEW LOOK FOR A NEW MILLENNIUM

Prior to the 2000 season, the Patriots unveiled both a new uniform design (shown on this media guide) and plans for a new stadium in Foxboro.

PATS GET THEIR MAN                    FRIDAY, JANUARY 28, 2000 · BOSTON HERALD

# Finally, it's Belichick

## Kraft, Patriots get their coach as war with Tuna comes to an end

By MICHAEL FELGER

FOXBORO — It was nearly three years ago today that television cameras caught Bob Kraft and Bill Belichick, both trapped squarely in the middle of a Bill Parcells power play, climbing into Kraft's car and driving out of the Foxboro Stadium parking lot.

Yesterday, after three years of acrimony and a 25-day coaching "search" featuring token candidates, courtroom dramas and stunning reconciliations, Kraft drove Belichick back into the Patriots' world. At 4:04 p.m., the pair climbed out of Kraft's car in front of the Pats' offices wearing bright smiles. Two hours later, Belichick was being announced as the 14th head coach — but not the general manager — of the New England Patriots.

"The border war," said Parcells, "is over."

Of course, the Pats paid for this detente. As compensation, the Pats sent the Jets their first-round pick this year (No. 16 overall) and exchanged late-round picks in 2001 and 2002. On Tuesday, Kraft was set to go ahead with other plans (i.e. Tom Donahoe and Dom Capers), but a call from Parcells that night led to Kraft's relenting on the first-round deal Wednesday. The deal was closed yesterday.

"I'm very appreciative of the Patriots and the confidence they showed in me to make the commitment they have," said Belichick, who has a handshake agreement with Kraft on a five-year contract worth what is believed to be more than $2 million a season. "I want to repay that commitment."

Left unanswered is the front-office situation. On the day Pete Carroll was fired, Jan. 3, the Pats asked the Jets seeking permission to speak to Belichick about their coach and general manager jobs. However, the issue was sidestepped yesterday, leading to speculation that ex-Pittsburgh boss Donahoe was still in the running for the GM position.

While sources close to Dona-

haps a better compensation deal.

"I don't blame him for not giving up a number one until this court case was closed," said Parcells. "Why would he?"

As for Belichick's staff, he said he had yet to finalize it. Jets offensive coordinator Charlie Weis is considered a shoo-in for the same position here, while the defensive coordinator job could go to an in-house candidate like Ray Hamilton. Parcells, the Jets' director of football operations, has given Weis and defensive assistant Eric Mangini permission to talk to other teams.

As for the Pats' long list of free agents, Belichick said he'd get cracking on that as well. "The shopping list is quite a long one," he said. "There are a lot of things that have to be done in a relatively short period of time."

The free agency period begins Feb. 11, and the player on the top of that list is safety Lawyer Milloy. Milloy is among the players who have lobbied for Belichick. "Hopefully we can get down to working on a new deal," said Milloy's agent, Ray Anderson.

After twisting in the wind for over three weeks, Belichick said he first got word of a Pats' deal when Parcells called him early yesterday morning. Belichick then spoke to Kraft at around 9:30 before getting in his car and making the drive up from New York. Kraft said the two then met at a "secret spot along the road" and then drove on to Foxboro.

Belichick appeared slightly nervous at the press conference, but was able to poke fun at himself for his last trip in front of the cameras. His resignation announcement from the Jets on Jan. 4 was an admitted disaster.

"Hopefully this press conference will go a little better than the last one I had," he said.

"The opportunity to be in coaching is something I wasn't sure I'd have as late as 24 hours ago. I'm extremely grateful to have the opportunity to have the chance to coach in the 2000 season."

Of all the developments in the

HANDSHAKE SEALS IT: Pats owner Robert Kraft welcomes Bill Belichick to the organization after Belichick was hired as head coach yesterday.                    STAFF PHOTO BY BILL BELKNAP

The *Boston Herald* announced the hiring of Bill Belichick as the Patriots' new head coach. New England had to forfeit a first-round draft choice to the New York Jets in exchange for Belichick's services.

# New England's Iron Man

*I*n 2001, the Patriots broke precedent and waived the five-year waiting period for induction to the team's Hall of Fame when they selected Bruce Armstrong as the 11th player so honored. During a halftime ceremony at Foxboro Stadium in the midst of the team's victory against the Indianapolis Colts, a capacity crowd gave the 14-year veteran a standing ovation. Not only was Armstrong recognized as the best Patriot offensive lineman since John Hannah, but he also retired as the franchise's iron man. He presently holds the record for most games played for the New England Patriots.

In remarks made to sportswriter Ron Hobson, Armstrong commented, "Somebody called it a meaningless record and maybe to them it was. But it meant everything to me because if you go by the idea that football players play football, then it means that I was a football player for a long time."

The average career of an NFL player is less than three seasons, and Armstrong more than quadrupled that while battling in the trenches at both right and left tackle. He was old school all the way, enduring four surgical reconstructions, one for each knee and shoulder. He suffered countless other injuries that could have warranted arthroscopic procedures had Armstrong not simply dismissed the option with a call for ice and an Ace bandage or two.

The worst of his many injuries came against the

*Bruce Armstrong stiff-arms Jackie Harris of the Vikings in the Patriots' dramatic 26–20 overtime win on November 13, 1994.*

*Offensive tackle Bruce Armstrong embraces team owner Robert Kraft at Foxboro Stadium. The Patriots honored the 14-year veteran and six-time Pro Bowl performer with the presentation of a framed jersey in honor of his selection to the team's Hall of Fame in 2001.*

Bills at Rich Stadium on November 1, 1992, when his right knee popped in a collision with Buffalo All-Pro defensive end Bruce Smith. Armstrong tore the medial collateral ligament, as well as both the anterior and posterior cruciate ligaments, of his knee. Several doctors recommended he retire, but Armstrong asked that it be repaired and endured an agonizing rehabilitation that saw him start once more the following season.

The 300-pounder was a team leader both on and off the field and kept most of his remarks in the locker room and off the sports pages. Like his former teammate Steve Grogan, Armstrong is remembered as much for his toughness as for his all-around excellence. In 2000, he was named to the Patriots' All-Century team, in addition to his earlier selection to the 35th anniversary team. He was also a member of six Pro Bowl squads.

# The Hiring of Coach Belichick

Within 24 hours of the Patriots' final game of the 1999 season, owner Robert Kraft fired head coach Pete Carroll and faxed the Jets a memo requesting permission to talk to them about Bill Belichick. Kraft, however, faced a major hurdle in hiring Belichick, since he was still under contract to the Jets as their defensive coordinator. In fact, Jets owner Leon Hess had given his valued assistant coach a cool million as a bonus for services rendered for the Jets' 1998 division championship. Implicit in the payment was an understanding that Belichick would succeed head coach Bill Parcells when the former Patriots boss decided to move upstairs.

Just as the Patriots were about to make their move on Belichick, Parcells quit his coaching duties and handed the reins, as well as his $1.4-million salary, to Belichick.

All hell broke loose, however, when Belichick formally announced his resignation as Jets head coach in a press conference.

*Patriots owner Robert Kraft* (right) *greets Bill Belichick at the press conference announcing Belichick's hiring as Patriots head coach on January 27, 2000.*

New York sportswriters speculated that Belichick must have already agreed in principle to a deal with New England.

In the days that followed, the surreal drama continued when Belichick sued the NFL to get out of his Jets contract. Finally, after NFL commissioner Paul Tagliabue ruled that Belichick's Jets contract was valid, Parcells picked up the phone and called his former boss in Foxboro.

At first, Robert Kraft thought he was the victim of a practical joke. When Parcells insisted his call was genuine, the men talked for nearly an hour. Not only did they mend fences, but they also came up with a blockbuster deal. The Patriots dealt their first-round pick in the 2000 draft (the 16th overall selection), along with fourth- and seventh-round picks, to the Jets for their fifth-round pick in 2001, seventh-round pick in 2002, and Belichick.

At the time, many doubted Kraft's sanity, but time has proven it may have been the best transaction in Patriots history.

## THE BORDER WAR

The so-called Jets/Patriots "Border War" has become an ongoing saga, aggravated in the late 1990s by the Jets' hiring of Parcells as head coach following the Patriots' Super Bowl season of 1996, as well as the Jets' free-agent signing of Curtis Martin in 1998. Things heated up again when the Patriots hired Bill Belichick in 2000, and once more with the defection of Patriot assistant coach Eric

*Martin escapes from Jet Mo Lewis.*

"Man-genius" Mangini to the Jets' head coaching job in January 2006. Soon, the absence of the postgame handshake between Belichick and Mangini became the symbol of the continuing rivalry.

# CHAPTER SIX

# The Brady Bunch

## 2000–TODAY

*"At this time in our country, we are all Patriots,*

*and tonight the Patriots are champions."*

**ROBERT KRAFT, AFTER NEW ENGLAND WON ITS FIRST SUPER BOWL ON FEBRUARY 3, 2002**

**Above:** *The Patriots' third Super Bowl triumph in four seasons is celebrated on their championship ring, which has three diamonds above their "Flying Elvis" icon. Each diamond represents one of their three Vince Lombardi Trophies.* **Right:** *Tom Brady launches a pass against the Jacksonville Jaguars. The Patriots overcame the Jags, 31–20, to advance in the 2007 AFC playoffs.*

# Rocky Road

The most important move of the Patriots' 2000 season was executed without a block, pass, or kick. No face-painted fans screamed their approval. No musket-firing colonial militia filled the end zone with the resounding crack of smoke-filled touchdown tribute volleys. In fact, the most significant act in recent Patriot history occurred long before the season had even kicked off, when the Patriots made their seventh of ten selections in the 2000 NFL Draft.

*In his final full season as the Patriots' quarterback in 2000, Drew Bledsoe was plagued by injuries and interceptions (13) and led the team to a dismal last-place finish in the AFC East.*

The 2000 draft was cast as a bit of a letdown for the Patriots, due to the fact that they had traded their first-round pick, 16th overall, to the Jets as compensation for the signing of new head coach Bill Belichick. By the time they had chosen tackle Adrian Klemm in the second round and running back J. R. Redmond in the third, all but the most devoted fans had resumed talking about the Red Sox.

By the time the Patriots reached the sixth round, their brain trust, led by Belichick and player personnel director Scott Pioli, consulted the draft tote board and once again reviewed the scouting report, which quarterback coach Dick Rehbein had filed. The report especially touted the skills of Michigan quarterback Tom Brady. So, with the 199th overall pick of the 2000 NFL Draft, the Patriots selected the player who would eventually lead them to the promised land.

The 2000 season proved a dud for the Patriots, who lost their first four games and eight of their first ten. The few highlights included road wins in Denver and Buf-

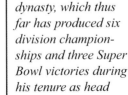

*Bill Belichick is the stoic mastermind behind the New England Patriots' dynasty, which thus far has produced six division championships and three Super Bowl victories during his tenure as head coach.*

falo and outstanding individual seasons for wide receivers Troy Brown (83 receptions) and Terry Glenn (79 receptions).

As the team floundered, Tom Brady sat as the fourth-string quarterback behind Drew Bledsoe, John Friesz, and Michael Bishop. During this time he studied the team's complex offense, which offensive coordinator Charlie Weis had crafted. Brady worked out with the intensity of a lineman, and, according to sportswriter Christopher Price, informed team owner Robert Kraft during an impromptu hallway encounter that he, Brady, was "the best decision this organization has ever made."

The team's final record of 5–11 was identical to that achieved by the Patriots during Bill Parcells's first season in 1993. Fans continued to fill Foxboro Stadium in the hope that their highly regarded coach and superstar quarterback could lead them back to the Super Bowl. After all, Drew Bledsoe was only 28 years old, and his best years were still ahead of him.

# Bledsoe's Triumph

After suffering a devastating hit in week two of the 2001 season in a game against the Jets, Drew Bledsoe was forced to watch the season unfold from the sidelines. Even after the former No. 1 pick and Pro Bowler had regained his health, head coach Bill Belichick decided to stick with backup quarterback Tom Brady, who had none of the lofty credentials that Bledsoe had accumulated.

Brady had split playing time in college at the University of Michigan, which led to him being selected as the 199th draft choice in 2000. In his rookie year, Brady completed only one pass, sitting on the bench as the team managed just five victories. Despite Brady's less than stellar past, however, he had quickly grown into the role of leader, and Belichick decided to stick with what was working.

Like any player would be, especially one who has had success, Bledsoe was emotionally hurt when he was replaced as the team's leader. Since his rookie year in 1993, Drew Bledsoe had become one of the better quarterbacks in the league and the reason for newfound optimism in New England. He had proven he could play the role of glamour-boy quarterback, but in the 2001 season, Bledsoe also proved he could be a great teammate.

Bledsoe quickly accepted his role as backup, and he became a mentor, coach, and fan of Tom Brady. Bledsoe was accustomed to helping the team off the field from his time spent injured, and he continued with that important

*Bledsoe is helped to his feet after sustaining a devastating body blow from Mo Lewis of the New York Jets.*

role throughout the season, easing Brady's transition to starting quarterback.

The Patriots continued their success in the first round of the playoffs, beating Oakland in the infamous snow game, and headed into Pittsburgh to battle for the AFC title. The Pats got off to a quick start on a punt returned for a touchdown by Troy Brown, but they faced more adversity in the second quarter. Tom Brady got sacked low, twisted his ankle, and was forced from the game. Luckily New England had the best second-string quarterback in the league ready to take over.

Drew Bledsoe revised his old role and turned potential disaster into excitement. In his first series in the game, Bledsoe rolled to his right, heading for the sidelines, and got hit with a tackle eerily similar to the one that knocked him out earlier in the season. But this time he jumped back up and was ready to play.

Shortly afterward, Bledsoe threw a touchdown pass to David Patten, making the score 14–3, and the Pats went into halftime with the lead. Bledsoe managed the game brilliantly, spreading the ball around and giving up no turnovers. The Pats withstood a late flurry by the Steelers and won the game 24–17, sending them to the Super Bowl.

Drew Bledsoe would never play again for the New England Patriots, but against the Steelers he lifted up his team one last time and truly earned his Super Bowl ring.

*Quarterback Drew Bledsoe displays the 2001 AFC championship trophy. In what was to be his final game for the Patriots, Bledsoe replaced an injured Tom Brady in the second quarter of the AFC title game and led the Pats to victory.*

# We Are All Patriots

As millions of Americans watched their fourth hour of Super Bowl pregame hyperbole and consumed yet another bratwurst, Tom Brady slept. A half hour prior to kickoff, the Patriots' wunderkind quarterback curled up for a catnap on the floor in a remote corner of the Superdome locker room, while teammates adjusted pads, huddled with coaches, or simply sat in silent prayer.

A California kid who had grown up in the Bay Area worshipping quarterback Joe Montana, Brady must have envisioned, as he napped, the type of performance his hero had delivered for the San Francisco 49ers in four previous Super Bowls. After all, the Patriots would need Brady to play the game of a lifetime.

The Patriots had come to New Orleans as 14-point underdogs against the St. Louis Rams, the highest pregame line since Joe Namath and the Jets lined up to play the Colts in 1969 as 17-point underdogs.

The Patriots set the tone for the game long before kickoff when they insisted on being introduced as a team rather than by the traditional recitation of the names of individual starters. The gesture was perfect for a squad that had faced preseason odds of 75–1 to win the Super Bowl.

For three quarters, the Patriots neutralized the Rams' vaunted attack, allowing only a first-quarter 50-yard field goal by Jeff Wilkins. The game's first touchdown came on a brilliant 47-yard interception return of a Kurt Warner pass by Patriot left cornerback Ty Law.

With a little more than a minute remaining in the first half, the Patriot defense again came up with a critical play. Just as Ram receiver Ricky Proehl caught a Warner laser over the middle of the field, Patriot Antwan Harris slammed into Proehl, causing the receiver to fumble the ball. Fellow Patriot defensive back Terrell Buckley scooped it up and ran to the Ram 40-yard line. And with just over 30 seconds to go in the half, Brady connected with his favorite receiver, David Patten, on a graceful timing route that saw Patten leap at the back of the end zone and

*The Patriots made a resounding pregame statement when they eschewed the traditional individual player introductions and ran onto the Louisiana Superdome playing field as a team.*

*Patriots cornerback Ty Law (No. 24) breaks up a pass intended for Rams wide receiver Torry Holt (No. 88) in the third quarter of Super Bowl XXXVI.*

snare the pass that gave New England a commanding 14–3 half-time lead.

After a prolonged halftime show that featured a moving tribute to the victims of 9/11 by U2, the Patriots continued their defensive mastery of the Rams. Patriot offensive coordinator Charlie Weis later remarked of Belichick: "Every year, no matter who he's playing, his players seem to know what the other team is doing before they do it. That's not by accident."

When Patriot cornerback Otis Smith picked off a Warner pass after Ram receiver Terry Holt slipped on the artificial turf, the Patriots marched downfield. Although the Rams finally stopped their drive, Vinatieri kicked a 37-yard field goal to increase the Patriots' lead to 17–3.

The Rams, however, stormed back. Warner scored on a keeper play that cut the Pats' lead to 17–10. Then, with just under two

minutes to play, the Rams tied the score on a three-play drive capped by a 26-yard Warner pass to Proehl.

In the broadcast booth, former Raiders coach and Super Bowl winner John Madden commented that Brady and the Patriots should manage their offense carefully for the final 81 seconds of the half and shoot for overtime. On the Patriot sideline, however, that notion was considered only briefly, as the brain trust of Weis and Belichick assessed the fact that they had zero timeouts with 83 yards to the Rams' end zone. Belichick's pithy response was also a slogan for the Patriots' unlikely season: "OK, let's go for it."

As time melted away on the Superdome clock, Brady completed five of six passes for 53 yards to set up Adam Vinatieri's 48-yard game-winning field goal. It marked the first championship title for the Patriot franchise and the first Boston pro sports title in 16 years.

When receiving the Vince Lombardi Trophy, team chairman Robert Kraft brushed away confetti and remarked, "The fans

of New England have been waiting 42 years. We are the world champions.... At this time in our country, we are all Patriots, and tonight the Patriots are champions."

*Patriots kicker Adam Vinatieri (No. 4) celebrates with holder Ken Walter as his 48-yard field goal splits the uprights to win Super Bowl XXXVI.*

# PATRIOTS PANORAMA

The Patriots' first Super Bowl triumph is featured on the front page of *The Boston Globe*.

Patriots players reach for the Holy Grail of professional football, the Vince Lombardi Trophy, on the occasion of their first-ever Super Bowl victory on February 3, 2002.

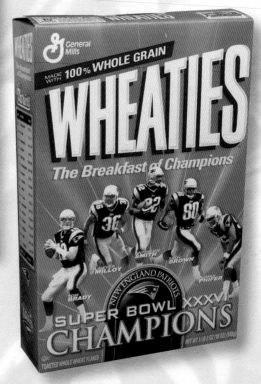

This Wheaties box spotlights the Super Bowl XXXVI champions and features Tom Brady, Lawyer Milloy, Antowain Smith, Troy Brown, and Roman Phifer.

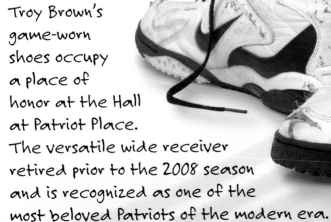

Troy Brown's game-worn shoes occupy a place of honor at the Hall at Patriot Place. The versatile wide receiver retired prior to the 2008 season and is recognized as one of the most beloved Patriots of the modern era.

Super Bowl XXXVI, highlighted in this program, marked both the Patriots' third trip to the NFL title game and their third trip to the Louisiana Superdome for the big game.

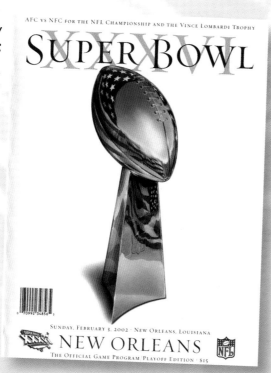

AFC vs NFC for the NFL Championship and the Vince Lombardi Trophy

# SUPER BOWL
## XXXVI

SUNDAY, FEBRUARY 3, 2002 · NEW ORLEANS, LOUISIANA

## NEW ORLEANS

The Official Game Program/Playoff Edition · $15

The Patriots' first Super Bowl ring displays their "Flying Elvis" logo, surrounded by numerous diamonds.

This 550-piece jigsaw puzzle, sold by White Mountain Puzzles, celebrates the Patriots' state-of-the-art home at Gillette Stadium.

NEW ENGLAND

550 PIECE PUZZLE

Photo by Mike Smith

WHITE MOUNTAIN PUZZLES INC.

Cornerback Ty Law, whose No. 24 jersey is seen here, anchored the Patriots' secondary for a decade, securing four Pro Bowl selections and a spot on the roster of the Patriots' All-Century team.

# A Super Celebration

The economy of New England suffered a brief nosedive on the afternoon of February 5, 2002, when more than a million citizens called in sick or took an extended coffee break in order to flock to the streets of Boston to celebrate the Patriots' Super Bowl triumph against the St. Louis Rams. Acting Massachusetts governor Jane Swift even gave all nonessential state employees an extra hour on their lunch breaks to attend the festivities.

The first carloads of fans arrived at dawn, with others jamming their way into subway cars for the trip to Beantown. Boston police closed most of the streets adjacent to the parade route by 11:00 A.M., so countless fans had to walk in large groups from remote parking lots and transit stops to join the festivities. They came from as far away as Skowhegan, St. Johnsbury, Block Island, Hampden County, and the Litchfield Hills, clad in silver paint and blue jerseys, toting air horns and cowbells, and carefully concealing bottles and flasks.

For some, the party had started more than a month earlier, following the Pats' first division title in five years. For others, it began the instant Adam Vinatieri tied Oakland with his miracle field goal in the dying seconds of their divisional thriller. But for most, the party had only just begun.

Such was the spirit of the celebration, unlike any seen in Boston before. *The Boston Globe* captured the essence of the day perfectly with the next day's banner headline, simply proclaiming: "Sea of Joy."

Much of what made the Patriots' first Super Bowl victory celebration extra special was the fact that fans had waited 42 years for a football world title—not to mention the 16 years that had passed since the Boston Celtics prompted a similar (yet much smaller) celebration.

Much had changed in Boston since the 1986 Celtics parade. The afterglow of their celebration had been quickly shattered

*Lawyer Milloy displays the Vince Lombardi Trophy at the rally at Boston's City Hall Plaza on February 5, 2002.*

when their first-round draft choice, Len Bias, died as the result of a cocaine overdose. That autumn, fans were further traumatized by recurring visions of that infamous ball rolling through Bill Buckner's legs as the Red Sox's first World Series win since 1918 evaporated in the chill of Shea Stadium. The Patriots, despite playing (and losing) their first Super Bowl just months earlier, were once again relegated to the status of laughingstock after a drug scandal rocked the team.

Fortunately, history was irrelevant for most of the throng that cheered the Patriots in early February 2002. Fans climbed up light poles and gathered at office windows to catch a glimpse of the parade—which included half the team and nearly all the executive and coaching staff—as it made its way from Government Center to City Hall Plaza.

*Patriots owner Robert Kraft* (left) *high-fives Ty Law* (right) *during the rally celebrating the Patriots' first Super Bowl victory.*

*Head coach Bill Belichick flashes a rare smile while posing with the Lombardi Trophy prior to Super Bowl XXXVI.*

At City Hall, safety Lawyer Milloy held the Lombardi Trophy aloft and shouted, "I love you guys. This is your trophy." Cornerback Ty Law then called out team owner Robert Kraft and quarterback Tom Brady and challenged them to bust a few dance moves. For many, the sight of Kraft gyrating joyously to a hip-hop beat was the highlight of the celebration. Brady, for his part, kept a low profile. Many speculated he did so consciously, out of respect for fellow quarterback Drew Bledsoe, who was the event's most conspicuous no-show.

For his part, Kraft survived his dance routine and received a thunderous ovation when he held the trophy aloft and remarked, "I grew up in this town, in this region. What you did for us today, we say thank you to you fans for everything you've done. I wanted to see in my lifetime a world championship come to this region. And today we're all world champions."

Belichick then noted to the joyous crowd, "We began this journey a long time ago in training camp. It's been six months. It's been a long journey and I feel like our journey's complete. Right now for these players, it's our time. They did it. Congratulations, champions."

# Home Sweet Home

*F*or 42 long seasons, generations of Patriots fans paid among the highest ticket prices in the NFL, endured the worst traffic jams, and suffered through decades of inept football action in the hope that their team would someday get things right. How sweet it was when they finally captured their first Super Bowl in 2002! And how sweet it continues to be in their new and incredible ever-growing stadium complex!

Rising from the rolling acres of south suburban Boston like the mast of a ship cresting an ocean wave, the light towers of Gillette Stadium cast a glow at once eerie and inspiring.

The transformation of Foxboro could not have been more complete had Pixar devised a virtual alternative football universe. With the opening of the Patriots' new home in 2002 and the subsequent debut of Patriot Place in 2008, the franchise that once seemed headed for St. Louis or Hartford had more than matched its football glory with an edifice for the ages.

When the Patriots finally decided to remain in Foxboro after a brief flirtation with the city of Hartford in 1998, the Kraft family envisioned the construction of not only a new stadium but also a massive retail and entertainment complex for their 350-acre parcel, which included the extremely outdated Foxboro Stadium. With zoning in place and the backing of the Commonwealth of Massachusetts for infrastructure upgrades, the New England Patriots poured the concrete for their new stadium's foundation on June 15, 2000.

While head coach Bill Belichick rebuilt the football team, the steel skeleton of the new stadium rose majestically alongside its humble ancestor. Fans soon forgave the new coach for the 5–11 record of his first year with the knowledge that both the team and stadium would soon represent a new era for the New England Patriots.

On January 19, 2002, fans bid farewell to Foxboro Stadium, enduring a blizzard that swirled as Adam Vinatieri kicked the

*Gillette Stadium glowed like a jewel on the night of its grand opening on September 9, 2002.*

*The opening of Gillette Stadium in 2002 coincided with the Patriots' first Super Bowl victory. Built adjacent to the site of Foxboro Stadium, the new stadium is the centerpiece of Patriot Place, a huge retail and entertainment complex.*

Patriots past the Raiders in the most memorable home game in franchise history. By spring, the new stadium, first christened as CMGI Field, opened its lower bowl for Revolution soccer games. The rest of the facility was readied for the NFL season to come.

On August 5, the stadium was renamed Gillette Stadium, with the company signing a 15-year naming agreement with the Krafts. One week later, the Patriots hosted the Philadelphia Eagles in an exhibition game that prompted rave reviews from fans who had tired of the years spent sitting on the uncomfortable aluminum benches that were a trademark of the now-demolished Foxboro Stadium.

The Patriots' new home was the perfect mix of form and function, and it offers as many amenities for the average fan as for the corporate luxury-suite tenant. Surrounded by nearly 17,000 parking spaces, Gillette Stadium seats 68,756, including 87 luxury suites and two massive super suites. The eight-story structure also features a giant HDTV screen measuring 48 by 27 feet above each end zone, 46 permanent concession stands, 60 portable concession stands, and more than 1,000 television monitors distributed throughout the stadium.

Among the other distinguishing features of the stadium is an arched pedestrian bridge at the west end, topped by a 12-story lighthouse with a beacon that radiates for miles across the region. Both structures pay homage to New England: The bridge imitates the colonial bridge at the battlefield green in Lexington, and the lighthouse pays tribute to the region's storied maritime heritage.

With the ongoing development of Patriot Place, a retail/entertainment cluster will soon surround the stadium. It already includes several restaurants, a cinema complex, a shopping plaza, and the Northeast's first-ever Bass Pro Shops store—complete with woodland and wetland trails.

When the team opened its Hall at Patriot Place in a corner of the stadium adjacent to their ProShop in 2008, it marked the third such museum in the NFL, after those of the Packers and Cowboys. Once again, the Patriots perfectly melded their competitive and commercial identities.

Adorned with three huge Super Bowl banners and a food court, Gillette Stadium has gone from sports shrine to year-round destination.

*Two of the main architectural features of Gillette Stadium are the lighthouse that marks the west end zone and the pedestrian bridge that spans the stadium's service entrance.*

# The Ultimate Patriot

Versatile, cheerful, tough, talented, and professional. All of these adjectives perfectly describe Patriots all-time great Troy Brown.

In his 15 seasons in Foxboro, Brown became as much a symbol of the Patriots as Pat Patriot or the Flying Elvis. His significance to the franchise stretches far beyond the realm of individual statistics or championships won, though his haul of three Super Bowl rings makes him one of a handful of Patriots so honored. His true greatness lay in his considerable football instincts, which allowed him to play virtually anywhere on the field in nearly any situation.

Like Tom Brady, Brown started his career as a late-round draft choice (eighth round, 198th overall selection) and as a backup. Beating the odds to make the roster of the 1993 squad, he cheerfully handled the thankless chore of punt returns for several seasons before finally blossoming into a wide receiver in 2000. He quickly established his credentials as a winner, emerging as a player whose versatility made him both an ideal and indispensable player for the creative genius of coach Bill Belichick.

Brown's 2001 season was incredible. He led the team with 101 receptions and the NFL in punt-return yardage, with an average return of 14.2 yards. Coach Belichick praised his star, stating, "Oh man, he is some football player. . . . You have to love guys like that on your team. He puts the team first. That's really a great example he sets for our younger players because he's so team oriented. A lot of things have come his way because of hard work and determination."

Upon his retirement prior to the start of the 2008 season, Brown was the Patriots' all-time leader in career receptions, with 557, and is currently the team career leader in punt returns, with 270, and punt-return yardage, with 2,625 yards. He also places eighth in team kickoff returns with 1,862 yards. In all, Brown led the team in receptions for three seasons and in punt returns for eight seasons.

At 5'10" and 193 pounds, Brown molded his extraordinary athleticism with an equal measure of heart and patience. In fact, Brown was waived and re-signed in his second season. He didn't start a game until his fifth year, and he only became a full-time starter in his eighth season.

*Wide receiver Troy Brown eyes the football as it lands in his hands. This 60-yard touchdown led to New England's 38–17 victory against the Colts on October 21, 2001.*

# Back to the High Life

*Tedy Bruschi leaps for joy during the Patriots' win against Buffalo on December 27, 2003. The victory gave the Pats the home field for the entirety of the AFC playoffs.*

In the wake of New England's incredible Super Bowl run in 2001, the 2002 Patriots endured a mediocre campaign that featured a killer midseason stretch in which they lost five of seven games and fell from contention. Despite the fact that the squad produced six Pro Bowl players, that season remains the odd-fitting piece in the Patriots' championship puzzle.

In stark contrast, the 2003 Patriots were nearly perfect after getting one extremely ugly game out of their system to start the season. Facing former teammates Drew Bledsoe and Lawyer Milloy in Buffalo for their season opener, the Patriots failed miserably in a 31–0 rout by the Bills. Not only was the score an embarrassment, but the juxtaposition of the recently cut Milloy with budget-conscious Patriot management also became a hot topic for Boston sportswriters.

All was forgotten in Philadelphia the following week, when the Patriots scored two first-half touchdowns off turnovers in a 31–10 win against the Eagles. After the game, Belichick commented, "We played better. We executed better. We scored in the red area and we played better defense in the red area. It's not that complicated."

Returning home for their Gillette Stadium opener, they beat the Jets by a score of 23–16—this despite the Jets sacking Tom Brady five times and outgaining the Patriots by 35 yards. As they headed to Washington, New England's injured list looked like a prospective Pro Bowl roster, with receiver David Patten and linemen Damien Woody and Adrian Klemm joining linebackers Ted Johnson and Mike Vrabel on the sidelines. Not surprisingly, the Pats lost that game 20–17.

With their season record at 2–2, the Patriots began a record-setting string of 21 consecutive victories by defeating the Tennessee Titans, 38–30, in Foxboro. The game was a classic because the lead changed hands seven times before Patriot cornerback Ty Law picked off a Steve McNair pass for a 65-yard touchdown to seal the victory.

The balance of the season was nothing short of magical, for Belichick's squad played to their opponents' weaknesses, winning big (38–34 against the Indianapolis Colts) and small (9–3 against the Cleveland Browns) while running the table. It was only fitting that the bookend for the division-winning season was a 31–0 victory against Buffalo in Foxboro—the same margin by which the Bills had beaten the Patriots in September. Revenge was sweet as Brady threw for four touchdowns while Bledsoe came up empty and was benched in the fourth quarter.

*Buffalo quarterback Drew Bledsoe receives a harsh homecoming in Foxboro on December 27, 2003, when Patriot Rodney Harrison sacks him with a brutal hit.*

141

# Remember the Titans

The Patriots' playoff opener against the Titans occurred on January 10, 2004, and it more than lived up to the hype surrounding a game that was a rematch of the Patriots' 38–30 win against the Titans in the fifth game of the season. Scheduled for Foxboro once again, the only difference seemed to be the frigid temperature, which hovered at 2 degrees for most of the night. Patriot chairman Robert Kraft later described it as "Patriot weather."

With their 12-game win streak on the line, the Patriots played their toughest game of the season. Just four minutes into the game, quarterback Tom Brady, confused by the Titans' defensive alignment, called a timeout. He subsequently fired a perfect touchdown pass to wide receiver Bethel Johnson for an early 7–0 lead.

The Titans answered with a late first-quarter, five-yard touchdown run by Chris Brown, which followed a roughing-the-passer penalty on Patriot defensive end Richard Seymour in the red zone. Later, the ever-reliable Adam Vinatieri missed a 44-yard field-goal attempt, but Patriot Rodney Harrison intercepted a pass on the very next play.

As the Patriots marched down the field, Brady converted a third-and-13 play by hitting Johnson with a flare pass and then throwing a perfect block that sprung his receiver for a 14-yard pickup. Later on the drive, Brady faced a third-and-two situation in which he rolled right out of the pocket for a three-yard gain. Two plays later, he handed off to back Antowain Smith for the go-ahead touchdown.

As fans huddled behind flasks and Styrofoam cups of coffee at halftime, the Titans enjoyed a respite from the freezing climate in their heated locker room. It must have served them well, for they tied the game in the third quarter when wide receiver Derrick Mason snagged a Steve McNair pass and ran 11 yards for a touchdown after breaking through an Asante Samuel tackle.

With a little more than four minutes remaining and the score at 14–14, Adam Vinatieri kicked a 46-yard field goal to give the Patriots their 13th straight win and yet another trip to the AFC championship game. "You throw a parka on. You get as many kicks in as you can on the side," Vinatieri later remarked. "Then you sit on the seat and try to stay warm. Then you go out and kick a rock-hard ball 46 yards through the dense, cold air so that, just maybe, your teammates will swarm around you and keep you from freezing."

*Patriots fans celebrate the bone-chilling 2-degree temperature at Gillette Stadium as they watch the Pats beat the Tennessee Titans by a score of 17–14 in their divisional playoff game on January 10, 2004.*

# Peyton Place

If Patriots fans had their fill of Peyton Manning and the endless array of television commercials featuring the Colts' affable quarterback, then the Patriots' defense was even more tired of hearing how the NFL co-MVP would lead the Colts to victory in Foxboro on January 18, 2004.

What gave way, however, was a Colt offense that had averaged nearly 40 points in its first two postseason victories against the Denver Broncos and the Kansas City Chiefs. What also gave way was a stylish quarterback, who ended up completing as many passes (three) to Patriot cornerback Ty Law as to his top wide receiver Marvin Harrison. In the snow-covered mud of Gillette Stadium, the Patriots more than lived up to the team mantra of "defending our house."

Leading up to their fourth consecutive conference title, the Patriots maintained a defensive posture that saw opponents score only 68 points in Foxboro over the course of the regular season. Added to this record-setting total was the fact that the Patriots had allowed only 36 points in the seven home games leading up to their AFC title clash with the Colts. Linebacker Willie McGinest captured his team's attitude perfectly when he was asked about their strategy against the Colts. He replied, "Bloody their nose up a little bit. Every play make contact with the receivers, the tight ends, the backs, whoever."

*Patriot quarterback Tom Brady hugs Colts quarterback Peyton Manning shortly after New England overcame Indianapolis to win the AFC champion- ship in the freezing confines of Gillette Stadium.*

On the other side of the ball, the Patriots took the opening kickoff and scored on their first drive. Tom Brady moved them 65 yards on 13 plays, including a fourth-down, two-yard run on his own 44. He tossed four passes to wide receiver David Givens in this drive, including the seven-yard touchdown grab.

When Manning attempted to counter, he led the Colts to the Patriots' 5-yard line before tossing the first of his four interceptions—this one to former teammate Rodney Harrison. Within minutes, the Pats drove to the Colts' 13, where Adam Vinatieri scored one of his five playoff field goals.

The Patriot defense continued to make Manning's outing a nightmare in the first half, as Ty Law snared the first of his three interceptions following the Patriots' kickoff. Brady then completed three passes for 42 yards while driving his team 52 yards through the snow toward yet another Vinatieri field goal. On their next drive, the Colts botched their first punt of the postseason when Justin Snow's snap soared over punter Hunter Smith's head and was kicked through the end zone to give New England a commanding 15–0 halftime lead.

In the second half, Indianapolis managed to regain their composure and outscore New England. Nevertheless, they were no match for one of the greatest defensive units in NFL history. The Patriots won, 24–14, capturing the AFC title once again.

# Sweet Carolina

*I*n the frigid winter of 2003–2004, New England was reeling from skyrocketing fuel costs and still feeling the sting of the Red Sox's playoff defeat at the hands of the hated Yankees the previous autumn. The Patriots' second Super Bowl victory proved the ideal antidote.

New England had won its last 12 regular-season games and two playoff games before arriving at Super Bowl XXXVIII. It had been ten weeks since the Patriots even trailed in a game, and some experts rated them among the top three NFL teams ever.

At Houston's Reliant Stadium, the Patriots faced a tough Carolina Panther team led by veteran quarterback Jake Delhomme. For most of the first half, both teams slugged it out in a defensive struggle that remained scoreless for nearly half an hour. Following a stretch during which Vinatieri missed a 31-yard field-goal attempt and soon after had a 36-yard attempt blocked, New England finally scored. With barely three minutes to go in the first half, Tom Brady drove his team 20 yards after a Richard Seymour

*Ball carrier Kevin Faulk, with the help of center Dan Koppen, charges into Panthers defensive tackle Brentson Buckner for a critical gain.*

*Carolina Panthers quarterback Jake Delhomme coughs up the football when Patriot Mike Vrabel blindsides him during Super Bowl XXXVIII.*

recovery of a Panther fumble. Brady capped the drive with a five-yard touchdown pass to wide receiver Deion Branch.

The remainder of the first half resembled nothing less than a human pinball game as both teams scored at will. The Panthers executed a 95-yard drive that ended with a Delhomme 39-yard touchdown pass to wide receiver Steve Smith. New England immediately answered with a six-play, 78-yard scoring drive that featured three Brady completions, including a five-yard touchdown pass to receiver David Givens. On the ensuing kickoff, the Patriots' squib kick backfired when Panther tight end Kris

Mangum snared the ball and ran it to his own 47. On the next play, halfback Stephen Davis sprinted 21 yards to set up kicker John Kasay's booming 50-yard field goal that reduced the Patriots' lead to four points at the half, with the score at 14–10.

The third quarter was almost identical to the first quarter, as both teams once again failed to score. Just as the quarter expired, however, New England put together an eight-play, 71-yard drive that included a 33-yard Brady pass to tight end Daniel Graham and a two-yard touchdown run by Antowain Smith at the start of the fourth quarter. Once again, the teams braced for one of the biggest scoring explosions in Super Bowl history.

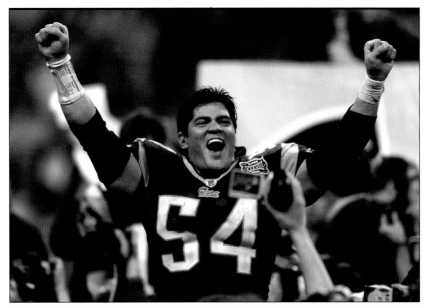

*Linebacker Tedy Bruschi celebrates the Patriots' victory against Carolina in Super Bowl XXXVIII at Reliant Stadium in Houston.*

and plunged into the end zone, giving the Patriots a 29–22 lead.

The Panthers once again struck back. Delhomme guided his team on a five-play touchdown drive that culminated in a 12-yard touchdown pass to wide receiver Ricky Proehl. Broadcasters were quick to point out that Proehl had also caught the late game-tying touchdown for the St. Louis Rams in the Patriots' last Super Bowl game, which was two years earlier.

Delhomme proved to be Brady's equal, directing the Panthers to the end zone courtesy of a pair of passes to Steve Smith and a 33-yard touchdown run by DeShaun Foster. Delhomme capped Carolina's scoring with an 85-yard pass to Muhsin Muhammad, the longest play in Super Bowl history at the time. It came after the Panthers intercepted Brady. The touchdown gave Carolina a 22–21 lead.

On their next series, the Patriots crafted a drive that showcased both Brady's skills and Belichick's uncanny football brain. After advancing 68 yards on a drive that included passes of 18 and 25 yards from Brady to wide receiver David Givens, the Patriots stunned the Panthers when linebacker Mike Vrabel lined up as an eligible tight end and scored on a one-yard toss from Brady. On the ensuing two-point conversion, running back Kevin Faulk took the direct snap

With a little more than a minute remaining, it appeared as though this might be the first Super Bowl to go into overtime. The Patriots, however, received a gift in the form of John Kasay's flubbed kickoff, which gave the Pats the ball on their own 40. Tom Brady once again summoned the spirits of Bart Starr and Joe Montana as he calmly completed four clutch passes to bring the Patriots to the Panthers' 23. Adam Vinatieri then kicked his second Super Bowl–winning field goal—with four seconds to spare. Unbelievable!

*The Patriots' win against the Carolina Panthers in Super Bowl XXXVIII is celebrated on this souvenir pennant, which features Tom Brady, Troy Brown, Tedy Bruschi, Rodney Harrison, Ty Law, Willie McGinest, Richard Seymour, and Adam Vinatieri.*

Because of his MVP heroics in Super Bowl XXXVIII, quarterback Tom Brady was featured on the cover of the February 9, 2004, issue of *Sports Illustrated*.

Tom Brady hoists the Vince Lombardi Trophy, with nearby teammate Antowain Smith posing for the cameras, after the Patriots' win in Super Bowl XXXVIII at Reliant Stadium in Houston, Texas.

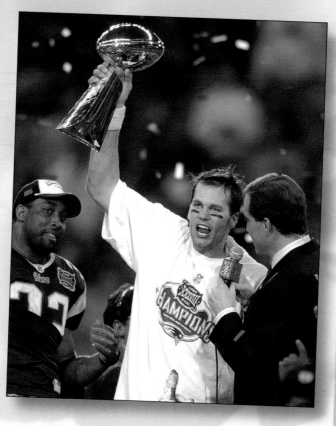

The Boston Globe proclaims the Patriots Super Bowl victors for a second time.

The Patriots' win against the Carolina Panthers in Super Bowl XXXVIII was a nail-biting affair. The two clubs are displayed on this popular 2004 pennant.

This miniature 2003 World Champions banner is a scale reproduction of the banner that hangs from the facade of Gillette Stadium.

A gigantic rendering of the Vince Lombardi Trophy is featured on the cover of this Super Bowl XXXVIII program.

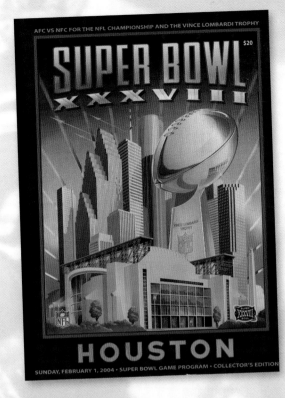

Patriots fans could celebrate the team's dynastic ascent by playing this collector's edition of the board game Monopoly.

The Patriots dynasty helped sell everything from breakfast cereal to beer. This poster used the Patriots to push Coors Light.

# 21 Up, 21 Down

*F*ootball historians will long debate the merits of the best of the Belichick-coached Patriot squads, and for many the 2004 team will rise to the top. They came close to running the table for a perfect season, losing only to the Steelers and Dolphins, both on the road. More important, the Patriots ran their streak of consecutive wins to 21 games, an NFL record, and sealed the deal with their third Super Bowl title in four seasons.

With two Super Bowl titles to their credit, the Patriots were regarded as the model franchise—not just for the NFL, but for all professional sports. In fact, their management model has been the basis for countless business school case studies, and their coaching staff a virtual training camp for future college and pro head coaches.

Opposing fans hated them as much as the Cowboys, Packers, Giants, Steelers, and other members of the NFL "royal family." Their ascendance was complete in every department, from their

*In action at the Edward Jones Dome, running back Corey Dillon leans toward the end zone while Rams defensive back Anthony Hargrove tries to push him out of bounds.*

*Patriots linebacker Mike Vrabel performs offensive duties against the Rams, catching a Tom Brady touchdown pass in St. Louis on November 7, 2004. The Patriots beat their former Super Bowl foes by a score of 40–22.*

Belichick brain trust of coaches and scouts to their state-of-the-art stadium.

The Patriots' home opener on September 9, 2004, was the perfect symbol of all that the team and the Kraft family had achieved in their first decade of ownership. Not only did the Pats face their bitter rivals, the Indianapolis Colts, but they did so while unfurling their second world championship banner, before a prime-time audience, with all the fanfare of the Super Bowl itself. As Brady paced impatiently in the Patriot locker room, fans were treated to a pregame concert that featured Lenny Kravitz, Toby Keith, Destiny's Child, and Kraft family friend Elton John.

In short time, Brady once more stole the show—with some help from linebacker Willie McGinest. While Brady connected on

26 of 38 passes with three touchdowns, the Patriot defense bailed the team out of a poor first half and later saved the game when McGinest sacked Colts quarterback Peyton Manning, forcing Colts kicker Mike Vanderjagt to miss the ensuing 47-yard field goal, his first miss in 43 attempts.

On the heels of their opening win, the Patriots marched through the schedule with relative ease before losing to Pittsburgh by a score of 34–20 at Heinz Field. They couldn't recover from the Steelers' 21-point first quarter, and their record-setting win streak ended at 21 games.

Over the remaining nine games of the regular season, the Patriots lost only one game, an agonizing one-point defeat to Miami. To the delight of Patriots fans, they captured their second consecutive AFC East crown and third in four seasons.

Included in this incredible run was an impressive 40–22 win against the Rams in St. Louis, during which Adam Vinatieri not only kicked four field goals but also tossed a four-yard touchdown pass to wide receiver Troy Brown in the third quarter. Linebacker Mike Vrabel once again displayed his versatility when he scored a touchdown on a two-yard pass from Brady in one of Belichick's patented eligible-receiver plays. Incredibly, Vrabel would score a second touchdown on the same kind of play in the regular-season finale versus the 49ers.

The 2004 team featured five Pro Bowl players, with special-teams ace Larry Izzo joining defensive lineman Richard Seymour, kicker Adam Vinatieri, linebacker Tedy Bruschi, and quarterback Tom Brady on the squad. Surprisingly, the Pro Bowl selectors left off newly acquired running back Corey Dillon, who had been simply sensational in 2004, recording the first 1,600-yard rushing season in the Patriots' 45-year history. With 1,635 yards, Dillon finished the 2004 season as the franchise's all-time single-season rushing leader.

While assessing his 2004 team, Belichick commented to *The Boston Globe,* "You just try to take the situation at hand and do the best you can with it. When it is over, recalibrate, reload, and go again. This is where we have been all season."

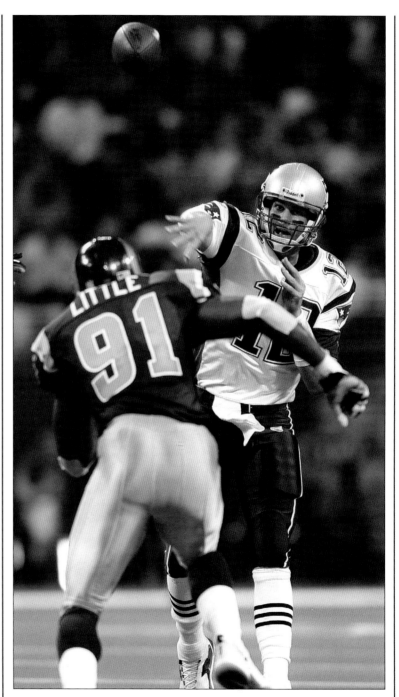

*Tom Brady, pressured by Leonard Little, launches a successful pass to Kevin Faulk in the first half of this contest between the Pats and Rams.*

# The Triple Crown!

The 2004 Patriots had only lost two games during the regular season, repeating their feat from 2003. One of the losses in '04 came against Miami, when Tom Brady had an unheard-of off day—yet New England still lost by only one point. The only team to truly outplay the Pats that season was the Steelers in week eight, but they more than made up for that setback by clobbering the Steelers in the AFC championship game, 41–27. In fact, it was a cakewalk for the Pats through the 2004 playoffs leading to Super Bowl XXXIX.

*Patriot linebacker Mike Vrabel dances like a bird in the end zone after scoring a touchdown. Teammate Stephen Neal (No. 61) rushes to hug him.*

Before defeating Pittsburgh, they had snuffed out Indianapolis, 20–3. The Patriots certainly earned their role as favorites to repeat in the Super Bowl.

Their opponents were the Philadelphia Eagles, who had finally made it to the big game after three straight failed attempts in the NFC championship game. The Eagles had taken a risk and added controversial All-Pro Terrell Owens to their group of wide receivers, which had produced little in the recent past. Their risk paid off that year, with Owens producing results and causing little trouble. The Eagles' offense hoped to exploit matchups between Owens and the Pats' secondary, which injuries had depleted. Meanwhile, the Eagles' strategy on defense relied on coordinator Jim Johnson's exotic blitzes to put pressure on Brady and disrupt his offense.

The beginning of the game featured stellar play by both defenses. Neither offense could find a rhythm, and the punters were brought out on the first few drives. The Eagles managed to get the ball inside the 20-yard line, thanks to a 30-yard catch by Owens, but quarterback Donovan McNabb tossed an interception to Patriot safety Rodney Harrison. Shortly afterward, the Eagles blew another chance when tight end L. J. Smith fumbled the ball and Pats cornerback Asante Samuel recovered.

The scoreless tie was finally broken about five minutes into the second quarter, when McNabb threw a short touchdown pass to Smith, making up for his earlier fumble. The play capped an 81-yard drive, which featured a 40-yard strike to receiver Todd Pinkston.

Two series later, the Pats took advantage of a short field after an Eagles punt and earned their first score of the game—with about a minute left in the first half—on a pass from Brady to wide receiver David Givens. The game stayed tied, 7–7, going into the second half.

*Tedy Bruschi rams quarterback Donovan McNabb into the ground in the Pats' victory against Philadelphia in Super Bowl XXXIX.*

The Pats used both their running backs on a fourth-quarter drive. Kevin Faulk, a versatile back, touched the ball three times, all for double-digit gains. Power runner and new addition Corey Dillon finished it with a two-yard touchdown run. New England then struck again, aided by a roughing-the-passer call against Philadelphia that set up Adam Vinatieri for a 22-yard field goal, putting the Patriots up, 24–14, with 8:43 to go in the game.

The Eagles' ensuing drive was thwarted by a Tedy Bruschi interception inside the Patriots' 25-yard line. After getting the ball back, McNabb led his team down the field but couldn't find a big play until a 30-yard connection with wideout Greg Lewis landed them in the end zone. The drive put them within three points, but it took 13 plays and 3:52 off the clock, leaving them with less than two minutes. The Pats then played it safe. They executed a smart blocking scheme to recover an onside kick attempt and ran three plays up the gut to burn Philly's timeouts. They got a great punt out of Josh Miller, leaving the Eagles 96 yards away from the end zone with only 46 seconds remaining.

With New England up, 24–21, the prayers of Eagles fans would not be answered. Questionable play calls left the Eagles scrambling in the middle of the field as time disappeared. On their third play, McNabb's pass attempt sailed right past the hands of L. J. Smith and into those of Rodney Harrison. The game was over, and the Patriots were champions once again.

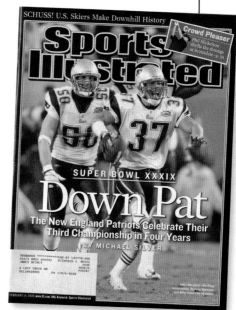

*Patriots Rodney Harrison and Mike Vrabel grace the cover of* Sports Illustrated. *This issue recounts the Patriots' exciting victory in Super Bowl XXXIX.*

*To the dismay of Eagles cornerback Lito Sheppard, Patriots wide receiver David Givens hauls in a touchdown pass in the second quarter of Super Bowl XXXIX at Alltel Stadium.*

In the third quarter, the teams again traded touchdowns. The opening drive by the Patriots resulted in a two-yard TD pass from Brady to Mike Vrabel, a linebacker whom the Patriots had used as a tight end in goal-line situations. Philadelphia had its own scoring drive late in the quarter, ending with a ten-yard pass to running back Brian Westbrook from McNabb. Going into the final quarter, the score was again tied—this time 14–14.

# PATRIOTS PANORAMA

Teammates Rabih Abdullah (left) and Larry Izzo (right) kiss the Vince Lombardi Trophy following the Patriots' narrow 24–21 squeaker against the Philadelphia Eagles in Super Bowl XXXIX.

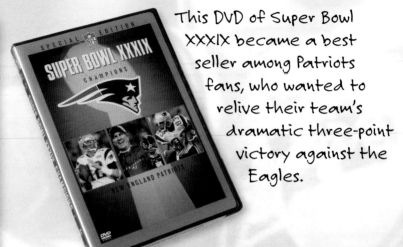

This DVD of Super Bowl XXXIX became a best seller among Patriots fans, who wanted to relive their team's dramatic three-point victory against the Eagles.

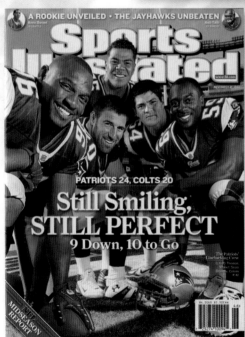

The Patriots' third Super Bowl victory in four seasons prompted *The Boston Globe* to declare them a dynasty.

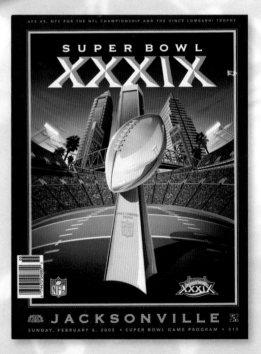

Following the Patriots' 24–20 win against the Colts on November 4, 2007, *Sports Illustrated* spotlighted their victory with this cover.

This Super Bowl XXXIX program set the stage for the Patriots' third NFL championship, which they claimed in Jacksonville, Florida, on February 6, 2005.

The Patriots' amazing journey to Super Bowl XLII is featured on this poster.

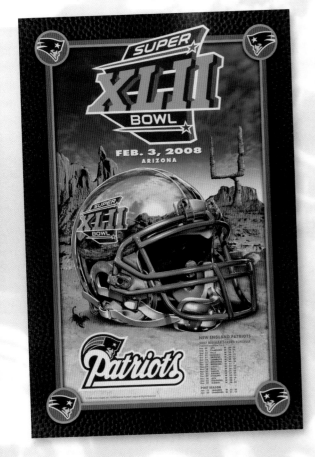

The 2007 Lamar Hunt Trophy recognized the Patriots' AFC championship victory. Their season was perfect until the Giants beat them in the Super Bowl.

Quarterback Tom Brady's 50 touchdown passes and wide receiver Randy Moss's 23 touchdown receptions highlighted the Patriots' perfect regular season in 2007, as displayed on this striking poster.

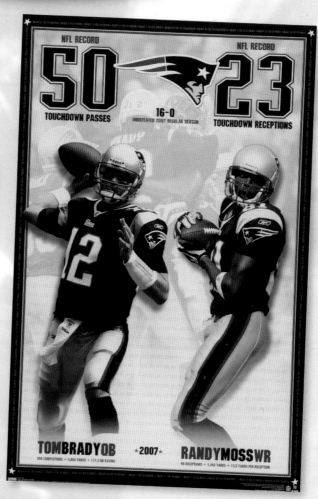

Wide receiver Randy Moss arrived in New England in 2007, after stints in both Minnesota and Oakland, and soon became a local hero. Moss is in a Patriots uniform in this popular bobblehead.

# Almost Perfect: The 2007 Patriots

After winning their third Super Bowl, New England succumbed to Denver, 27 13, the following season in the 2005 AFC playoffs, and to Indianapolis, 38–34, the year after that in the 2006 AFC championship game. Despite these painful losses, the Patriots had high hopes for the 2007 season, and for the regular season the Pats did not disappoint, going a perfect 16–0, a feat never accomplished before by an NFL team in a 16-game season.

Patriots fans, however, learned the full meaning of "almost" when the 2007 squad lost in the Super Bowl after skating through the AFC playoffs. At approximately 9:49 P.M. (EST) on February 3, 2008, with 35 seconds remaining in Super Bowl XLII, New York Giants quarterback Eli Manning and wide receiver Plaxico Burress collaborated to paint a mustache on the Mona Lisa that was to be the Patriots' perfect season. For it was Manning's arching touchdown toss to an outstretched Burress that capped a 12-play, 83-yard Giants scoring drive, one that also included David Tyree's impossible third-down reception. That touchdown spoiled what would have been the greatest season in NFL history.

For the record, the 2007 Patriots became the first North American major-league pro sports franchise since 1884 to win their first 18 games. They outscored regular-season opponents by a whopping margin of 589 to 274 points. Quarterback Tom Brady gained even greater fame for setting a league and franchise record with 50 touchdown passes, while also capturing the NFL's Most Valuable Player Award.

Beyond statistics, the true measure of greatness for the 2007 Patriots was the degree to which they assumed the role of public enemy to legions of jealous fans across the continent. The lingering aroma of the "Spygate" allegations, along with the subsequent fines and penalties levied against the team, placed the Patriots in that hallowed "timeout" corner of American sports occupied by the likes of the Raiders, Yankees, Mark Cuban, A-Rod, and John Daly, among others.

If only the one had come before any of the 18.

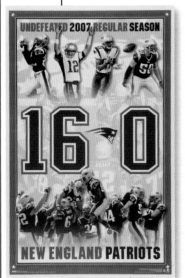

*The Patriots' perfect regular season in 2007 is celebrated on this poster.*

*Bill Belichick has proven a worthy successor to such NFL coaching legends as Vince Lombardi, Paul Brown, and Bill Walsh, leading the Patriots to three Super Bowl titles through the 2008 season.*

## SPYGATE

When it was revealed that the Patriots had violated NFL rules by taping the Jets' defensive formations, it unleashed a media storm that led to NFL commissioner Roger Goodell's office and all the way to the United States Senate. Ultimately, the Patriots and head coach Bill Belichick paid a steep price, for the league punished the team with the loss of their 2008 first-round draft choice and Belichick himself with a $500,000 fine. Later, when former team video assistant Matt Walsh alleged further (unproven) illegal videotaping, Senator Arlen Specter of Pennsylvania called for hearings while Goodell, for his part, considered the matter closed.

# The Superstar Quarterback

In the 2000 NFL Draft, 198 players were chosen before Tom Brady—a lanky, unproven quarterback from the University of Michigan. Brady's story involves luck, and possibly fate, but certainly proves that people can control their own destiny.

Brady did not get much attention from college scouts while at Junipero Serra High School in San Mateo, California, so he and his father put together a video of Tom and sent it to dozens of Division I football programs across the country. The University of Michigan was persuaded to let Brady on the team, but he still had to fight for playing time and ended up at the bottom of the draft.

As a rookie and third-string quarterback, Brady's role on the Pats did not faze him. He took everything he did seriously, and he showed signs of leadership early on in practice. Brady had a practical confidence, one which allowed him to play with poise but also left him with the desire to become better.

Circumstances made Brady a starter in 2001, after Drew Bledsoe went down with an injury, but he stayed there even when Bledsoe was healthy again because of his great success on the playing field.

Brady benefited from personnel decisions by Bill Belichick and player personnel director Scott Pioli, but he remained the keystone of the team and led them to the franchise's only three Super Bowl wins—and this in just four years of starting. The perennial bad luck of the New England Patriots seemed to balance itself out with four years of tremendous good fortune, putting Tom Brady on the short list of Boston sports legends, a list which includes the likes of Ted Williams, Bobby Orr, and Larry Bird.

Brady had the good fortune of being with the Patriots at the right time and with the perfect coach, but he paved his own road to greatness with hard work, intelligence, and confidence. Not only has he piled up incredible statistics, but Tom Brady has always been a winner, and he has never given less than his all for the New England Patriots.

*Tom Brady scores his first-ever regular-season rushing touchdown on December 16, 2002.*

## THE FALLEN HERO

*Tom Brady*

In 2008, Brady sat out the entire preseason to nurse nagging ankle, shoulder, and groin injuries, but he looked to be healthy for the regular season. Less than ten minutes into the Patriots' home opener against Kansas City, however, Brady was put right back on the disabled list, this time out for the whole season. Chiefs safety Bernard Pollard had hit Brady low, twisting his knee inward and tearing his medial collateral and anterior cruciate ligaments.

Although Brady did not play for the Patriots in 2008, the Pats finished their regular season with an 11–5 record. Despite a better record than three playoff teams and tying for first with the Miami Dolphins in the AFC East, New England did not make the 2008 playoffs. One can only wonder how far the Patriots would have gone had Brady been at the helm.

*In 2007, the Associated Press recognized quarterback Tom Brady as the NFL's Most Valuable Player and presented him with this trophy.*

# CHAPTER SEVEN

# Patriots by the Numbers

## SEASON RECORDS, 1960–2008

| Year | W | L | T | Standing |
|------|---|---|---|----------|
| 1960 | 5 | 9 | 0 | 4th |
| 1961 | 9 | 4 | 1 | 2nd |
| 1962 | 9 | 4 | 1 | 2nd |
| 1963 | 7 | 6 | 1 | AFL Eastern Division champion |
| 1964 | 10 | 3 | 1 | 2nd |
| 1965 | 4 | 8 | 2 | 3rd |
| 1966 | 8 | 4 | 2 | 2nd |
| 1967 | 3 | 10 | 1 | 5th |
| 1968 | 4 | 10 | 0 | 4th |
| 1969 | 4 | 10 | 0 | 3rd |
| 1970 | 2 | 12 | 0 | 5th |
| 1971 | 6 | 8 | 0 | 3rd |
| 1972 | 3 | 11 | 0 | 5th |
| 1973 | 5 | 9 | 0 | 3rd |
| 1974 | 7 | 7 | 0 | 3rd |
| 1975 | 3 | 11 | 0 | 4th |
| 1976 | 11 | 3 | 0 | 2nd |
| 1977 | 9 | 5 | 0 | 3rd |
| 1978 | 11 | 5 | 0 | 1st |
| 1979 | 9 | 7 | 0 | 2nd |
| 1980 | 10 | 6 | 0 | 2nd |
| 1981 | 2 | 14 | 0 | 5th |
| 1982 | 5 | 4 | 0 | 7th |
| 1983 | 8 | 8 | 0 | 2nd |
| 1984 | 9 | 7 | 0 | 2nd |
| 1985 | 11 | 5 | 0 | 2nd/AFC champions |
| 1986 | 11 | 5 | 0 | 1st |
| 1987 | 8 | 7 | 0 | 2nd |
| 1988 | 9 | 7 | 0 | 2nd |
| 1989 | 5 | 11 | 0 | 4th |
| 1990 | 1 | 15 | 0 | 5th |
| 1991 | 6 | 10 | 0 | 4th |
| 1992 | 2 | 14 | 0 | 5th |
| 1993 | 5 | 11 | 0 | 4th |
| 1994 | 10 | 6 | 0 | 2nd |
| 1995 | 6 | 10 | 0 | 4th |
| 1996 | 11 | 5 | 0 | 1st/AFC champions |
| 1997 | 10 | 6 | 0 | 1st |
| 1998 | 9 | 7 | 0 | 4th |
| 1999 | 8 | 8 | 0 | 4th |
| 2000 | 5 | 11 | 0 | 5th |
| 2001 | 11 | 5 | 0 | 1st/Super Bowl champions |
| 2002 | 9 | 7 | 0 | 2nd |
| 2003 | 14 | 2 | 0 | 1st/Super Bowl champions |
| 2004 | 14 | 2 | 0 | 1st/Super Bowl champions |
| 2005 | 10 | 6 | 0 | 1st |
| 2006 | 12 | 4 | 0 | 1st |
| 2007 | 16 | 0 | 0 | 1st/AFC champions |
| 2008 | 11 | 5 | 0 | 2nd |

## PLAYOFF GAMES

|  |  |  |
|------|-------|--------|
| December 28, 1963 | AFL Divisional | New England 26, Buffalo 8 |
| January 5, 1964 | AFL Championship | San Diego 51, New England 10 |
| December 18, 1976 | AFC Divisional | Oakland 24, New England 21 |
| December 31, 1978 | AFC Divisional | Houston 31, New England 14 |
| January 8, 1983 | First Round Playoff | Miami 28, New England 13 |
| December 28, 1985 | AFC Wild Card | New England 26, New York Jets 14 |
| January 5, 1986 | AFC Divisional | New England 27, Los Angeles Raiders 20 |
| January 12, 1986 | AFC Championship | New England 31, Miami 14 |
| January 26, 1986 | Super Bowl XX | Chicago 46, New England 10 |
| January 4, 1987 | AFC Divisional | Denver 22, New England 17 |
| January 1, 1995 | AFC Wild Card | Cleveland 20, New England 13 |
| January 5, 1997 | AFC Divisional | New England 28, Pittsburgh 3 |
| January 12, 1997 | AFC Championship | New England 20, Jacksonville 6 |
| January 26, 1997 | Super Bowl XXXI | Green Bay 35, New England 21 |
| December 28, 1997 | AFC Wild Card | New England 17, Miami 3 |
| January 3, 1998 | AFC Divisional | Pittsburgh 7, New England 6 |
| January 3, 1999 | AFC Wild Card | Jacksonville 25, New England 10 |
| January 19, 2002 | AFC Divisional | New England 16, Oakland 13 (OT) |
| January 27, 2002 | AFC Championship | New England 24, Pittsburgh 17 |
| February 3, 2002 | Super Bowl XXXVI | New England 20, St. Louis 17 |
| January 10, 2004 | AFC Divisional | New England 17, Tennessee 14 |
| January 18, 2004 | AFC Championship | New England 24, Indianapolis 14 |
| February 1, 2004 | Super Bowl XXXVIII | New England 32, Carolina 29 |
| January 16, 2005 | AFC Divisional | New England 20, Indianapolis 3 |
| January 23, 2005 | AFC Championship | New England 41, Pittsburgh 27 |
| February 6, 2005 | Super Bowl XXXIX | New England 24, Philadelphia 21 |
| January 7, 2006 | AFC Wild Card | New England 28, Jacksonville 3 |
| January 14, 2006 | AFC Divisional | Denver 27, New England 13 |
| January 7, 2007 | AFC Wild Card | New England 37, New York Jets 16 |
| January 14, 2007 | AFC Divisional | New England 24, San Diego 21 |

| January 21, 2007 | AFC Championship | Indianapolis 38, New England 34 |
| January 12, 2008 | AFC Divisional | New England 31, Jacksonville 20 |
| January 20, 2008 | AFC Championship | New England 21, San Diego 12 |
| February 3, 2008 | Super Bowl XLII | New York Giants 17, New England 14 |

## PATRIOTS OWNERS

| 1960–88 | William H. Sullivan |
| 1988–92 | Victor Kiam |
| 1992–94 | James Busch Orthwein |
| 1994–present | The Kraft Family |

## PATRIOTS HEAD COACHES

| 1960–61 | Lou Saban | 7–12–0 |
| 1961–68 | Mike Holovak | 53–47–9 |
| 1969–70 | Clive Rush | 5–16–0 |
| 1970–72 | John Mazur | 9–21–0 |
| 1972 | Phil Bengtson | 1–4–0 |
| 1973–78 | Chuck Fairbanks | 46–41–0 |
| 1978 | Hank Bullough | 0–1–0 |
| 1978–81 | Ron Erhardt | 21–27–0 |
| 1982–84 | Ron Meyer | 18–16–0 |
| 1984–89 | Raymond Berry | 51–41–0 |
| 1990 | Rod Rust | 1–15–0 |
| 1991–92 | Dick MacPherson | 8–24–0 |
| 1993–96 | Bill Parcells | 34–34–0 |
| 1997–99 | Pete Carroll | 28–23–0 |
| 2000–present | Bill Belichick | 116–45–0 |

## PATRIOTS HOME STADIUMS

| 1960–62 | Nickerson Field (at Boston University) |
| 1963–68 | Fenway Park |
| 1967 | San Diego Stadium (one game) |
| 1968 | Legion Field, Birmingham, Alabama (one game) |

| 1969 | Alumni Stadium (at Boston College) |
| 1970 | Harvard Stadium |
| 1971–82 | Schaefer Stadium (a.k.a. Foxboro Stadium) |
| 1983–89 | Sullivan Stadium (a.k.a Foxboro Stadium) |
| 1990–2002 | Foxboro Stadium |
| 2002–present | Gillette Stadium |

## MOST PRO BOWL APPEARANCES

| 9 | John Hannah (1976, 1978–85) |
| 7 | Jon Morris (1964–70) |
| 6 | Houston Antwine (1963–68) |
| 6 | Bruce Armstrong (1990–91, 1994–97) |
| 6 | Mike Haynes (1976–80, 1982) |

## MOST CONSECUTIVE PRO BOWL APPEARANCES

| 8 | John Hannah (1978–85) |
| 7 | Jon Morris (1964–70) |
| 6 | Houston Antwine (1963–68) |
| 5 | Ben Coates (1994–98) |
| 5 | Mike Haynes (1976–80) |
| 5 | Richard Seymour (2002–2006) |
| 5 | Andre Tippett (1984–88) |

## RETIRED NUMBERS

| 20 | Gino Cappelletti, K/WR (1960–70) |
| 40 | Mike Haynes, CB (1976–82) |
| 57 | Steve Nelson, LB (1974–87) |
| 73 | John Hannah, G (1973–85) |
| 78 | Bruce Armstrong, OT (1987–2000) |
| 79 | Jim Lee Hunt, DL (1960–71) |
| 89 | Bob Dee, DL (1960–67) |

*Patriots bobblehead*

## PATRIOTS IN THE PRO FOOTBALL HALL OF FAME

John Hannah (inducted in 1991)

Mike Haynes (inducted in 1997)

Nick Buoniconti (inducted in 2001)

Andre Tippett (inducted in 2008)

## PATRIOTS HALL OF FAME

John Hannah, G (1973–85; inducted in 1991)

Nick Buoniconti, LB (1962–68; inducted in 1992)

Gino Cappelletti, K/WR (1960–70; inducted in 1992)

Bob Dee, DL (1960–67; inducted in 1993)

Jim Lee Hunt, DL (1960–71; inducted in 1993)

Steve Nelson, LB (1974–87; inducted in 1993)

Babe Parilli, QB (1961–67; inducted in 1993)

Mike Haynes, CB (1976–82; inducted in 1994)

Steve Grogan, QB (1975–90; inducted in 1995)

Andre Tippett, LB (1982–93; inducted in 1999)

Bruce Armstrong, OT (1987–2000; inducted in 2001)

Stanley Morgan, WR (1977–89; inducted in 2007)

Ben Coates, TE (1991–99; inducted in 2008)

## SPECIAL AWARDS

### SPORTING NEWS AFL MOST VALUABLE PLAYER

1964    Gino Cappelletti, K/WR (also named UPI AFL Player of the Year)

1966    Jim Nance, FB (also named AP and UPI AFL Player of the Year)

### SUPER BOWL MVP AWARD

Super Bowl XXXVI—Tom Brady, QB

Super Bowl XXXVIII—Tom Brady, QB

### NFL OFFENSIVE PLAYER OF THE YEAR

2007    Tom Brady, QB

## NFL OFFENSIVE ROOKIE OF THE YEAR

### (NAMED BY THE ASSOCIATED PRESS)

1988    John Stephens, RB

1991    Leonard Russell, RB

1995    Curtis Martin, RB

## NFL DEFENSIVE ROOKIE OF THE YEAR

### (NAMED BY THE ASSOCIATED PRESS)

1976    Mike Haynes, CB

2008    Jerod Mayo, LB

## NFL COMEBACK PLAYER OF THE YEAR

### (NAMED BY THE ASSOCIATED PRESS)

2005    Tedy Bruschi, LB

## AFL COACH OF THE YEAR

1964    Mike Holovak

1966    Mike Holovak

## AFC COACH OF THE YEAR

1976    Chuck Fairbanks

1985    Raymond Berry

1994    Bill Parcells

## NFL COACH OF THE YEAR

2003    Bill Belichick

2007    Bill Belichick

## AFL ROOKIE OF THE YEAR

1969    Carl Garrett, RB

## NFL MOST VALUABLE PLAYER

2008    Tom Brady, QB

*Tom Brady 2005 button*

# PATRIOTS ALL-TIME LEADERS: PASSING
## (BASED ON PASSING YARDAGE)

| Name | Years | Att | Comp | Yards | Pct | TD | INT |
|---|---|---|---|---|---|---|---|
| 1. Drew Bledsoe | 1993-2001 | 4,518 | 2,544 | 29,657 | 56.3 | 166 | 138 |
| 2. Steve Grogan | 1975-90 | 3,593 | 1,879 | 26,886 | 52.3 | 182 | 208 |
| **3. Tom Brady** | **2000-2008** | **3,653** | **2,301** | **26,446** | **63.0** | **197** | **86** |
| 4. Vito "Babe" Parilli | 1961-67 | 2,412 | 1,140 | 16,747 | 47.3 | 132 | 138 |
| 5. Tony Eason | 1983-89 | 1,500 | 876 | 10,732 | 58.4 | 60 | 48 |
| 6. Jim Plunkett | 1971-75 | 1,503 | 729 | 9,932 | 48.5 | 62 | 87 |
| 7. Hugh Millen | 1991-92 | 612 | 370 | 4,276 | 60.5 | 17 | 28 |
| 8. Mike Taliaferro | 1968-70 | 680 | 305 | 3,920 | 44.9 | 27 | 44 |
| 9. Butch Songin | 1960-61 | 604 | 285 | 3,905 | 47.2 | 36 | 24 |
| 10. Matt Cavanaugh | 1978-82 | 385 | 206 | 3,018 | 53.5 | 19 | 23 |

# PATRIOTS ALL-TIME LEADERS: RUSHING
## (BASED ON RUSHING YARDAGE)

| Name | Years | Carries | Yards | Avg | LG | TD |
|---|---|---|---|---|---|---|
| 1. Sam Cunningham | 1973-79, 1981-82 | 1,385 | 5,453 | 3.9 | 75t | 43 |
| 2. Jim Nance | 1965-71 | 1,323 | 5,323 | 4.0 | 65t | 45 |
| 3. Tony Collins | 1981-87 | 1,191 | 4,647 | 3.9 | 54 | 32 |
| 4. Curtis Martin | 1995-97 | 958 | 3,799 | 4.0 | 70t | 32 |
| 5. Don Calhoun | 1975-81 | 820 | 3,391 | 4.1 | 73 | 23 |
| 6. John Stephens | 1988-92 | 891 | 3,249 | 3.6 | 52 | 17 |
| 7. Corey Dillon | 2004-2006 | 753 | 3,180 | 4.2 | 50 | 37 |
| **8. Kevin Faulk** | **1999-2008** | **777** | **3,170** | **4.1** | **45t** | **14** |
| 9. Larry Garron | 1960-68 | 763 | 2,981 | 3.9 | 85t | 14 |
| 10. Antowain Smith | 2001-2003 | 721 | 2,781 | 3.9 | 44 | 21 |

# PATRIOTS ALL-TIME LEADERS: RECEIVING
## (BASED ON NUMBER OF RECEPTIONS)

| Name | Years | No. | Yards | Avg | LG | TD |
|---|---|---|---|---|---|---|
| 1. Troy Brown | 1993-2007 | 557 | 6,366 | 11.4 | 82t | 31 |
| 2. Stanley Morgan | 1977-89 | 534 | 10,352 | 19.4 | 76t | 67 |
| 3. Ben Coates | 1991-99 | 490 | 5,471 | 11.2 | 82t | 50 |
| **4. Kevin Faulk** | **1999-2008** | **381** | **3,304** | **8.7** | **52t** | **14** |
| 5. Irving Fryar | 1984-92 | 363 | 5,726 | 15.8 | 80t | 38 |
| 6. Terry Glenn | 1996-2001 | 329 | 4,469 | 14.2 | 86t | 22 |
| 7. Gino Cappelletti | 1960-70 | 292 | 4,589 | 15.7 | 63t | 42 |
| 8. Jim Colclough | 1960-68 | 283 | 5,001 | 17.7 | 78t | 39 |
| 9. Tony Collins | 1981-87 | 261 | 2,356 | 9.0 | 49 | 12 |
| 10. Vincent Brisby | 1993-99 | 217 | 3,142 | 14.5 | 72 | 14 |

# PATRIOTS ALL-TIME LEADERS: INTERCEPTIONS
## (BASED ON NUMBER OF INTERCEPTIONS)

*boldface=still active*
*t=touchdown*

| Name | Years | No. | Yards | Avg | LG | TD |
|---|---|---|---|---|---|---|
| 1. Ty Law | 1995-2004 | 36 | 583 | 16.2 | 65t | 6 |
| 2. Raymond Clayborn | 1977-89 | 36 | 555 | 15.4 | 85 | 1 |
| 3. Ron Hall | 1961-67 | 29 | 476 | 16.4 | 87 | 1 |
| 4. Fred Marion | 1982-91 | 29 | 457 | 15.8 | 83 | 1 |
| 5. Roland James | 1980-90 | 29 | 383 | 13.2 | 46 | 0 |
| 6. Mike Haynes | 1976-82 | 28 | 393 | 14.0 | 50 | 1 |
| 7. Maurice Hurst | 1989-95 | 27 | 263 | 9.7 | 36 | 1 |
| 8. Ronnie Lippett | 1984-91 | 24 | 420 | 17.5 | 73 | 2 |
| 9. Nick Buoniconti | 1962-68 | 24 | 223 | 9.3 | 41 | 0 |
| **10. Asante Samuel** | **2003-2007** | **22** | **313** | **14.2** | **55t** | **3** |

# INDEX